W9-BHO-924

ISBN-13: 978-1-4351-1027-4

Published exclusively for Metro Books by Gusto Company AS

© 2006 JW Cappelens Forlag under license from Gusto Company AS

Written by Anna Mantzaris

Executive editor: James Tavendale

Edited by Katherine Robinson and Rachel Elliot

Original concept by James Tavendale and Ernesto Gremese

Edited by Katherine Robinson and Rachel Elliot

Designed by Allen Boe

Printed and bound in China

3 5 7 9 10 8 6 4 2

1001 THINGS YOU DIDN'T KNOW YOU WANTED TO KNOW

Anna Mantzaris

METRO BOOKS
NEW YORK

INTRODUCTION

From annoying clichés to electoral vote counts, here is a trivia book that eclipses all others. It isn't full of just the conventional trivia you might expect to find everywhere else.

Instead, it has all the stuff that you didn't even know that you wanted to know. Fortunately, we have made it our business to know what you didn't know that you wanted to know in order to include it in this book.

Choosing material that we anticipate you didn't know you wanted to know was a significant challenge. We were required to make a distinction between four things: stuff you wanted to know, and knew you wanted to know; things that you didn't know, but knew you didn't know and didn't want to; things you didn't know, didn't know you didn't know, but wouldn't want to know if you did; and, most elusive of all, things you didn't know you even wanted to know, but would soon discover that you wanted to, once you knew them. It is this stuff that appears in this book.

If there is anything that you feel strongly that you now know you didn't know you wanted to know that isn't here—please let us know.

CONTENTS

TELEVISION

The Cosby Show ran on NBC for eight seasons (1984-1992).
The Huxtable Kids on the show were:
Sondra
Denise
"Theo" (Theodore)
Vanessa
Rudy

Remember the popular television show **The Waltons** (1972-1981), set in the Blue Ridge Mountains of Virginia? Can you name all of the family members?
Zebulon Walton (grandfather)
Esther Walton (grandmother)
John Walton (father)
Olivia Walton (mother)
John Walton Junior (eldest son, known as John Boy)
Jason Walton (son)
Mary-Ellen Walton Willard Jones (eldest daughter)
Ben Walton (son)
Erin Esther Walton Northridge (daughter)
James Robert Walton (youngest son, known as Jim-Bob)
Elizabeth Walton

The first **Miss World** competition took place in 1951. The winner was Kiki Haakonson from Sweden. Laura Ellison-Davies (from the U.K.) was the first runner up.

Cable television was first introduced in Pennsylvania in 1948.

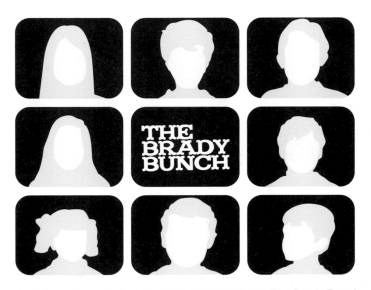

Just who belonged to television's All-American family, **The Brady Bunch** (1969-1974)?

Carol (mother)
Mike (father)
Greg (oldest son)
Marcia (oldest daughter)
Peter (son)
Jan (daughter)
Bobby (youngest son)
Cindy (youngest daughter)

Actress **Demi Moore** starred on ABC's long-running soap opera **General Hospital**.

WHERE IT HAPPENS: FICTIONAL SETTINGS FOR DAY-TIME TELEVISION SOAP OPERAS:

SOAP OPERA	FICTIONAL TOWN
General Hospital	Port Charles
All My Children	Pine Valley
One Life to Live	Llanview
The Young and the Restless	Genoa City
The Bold and the Beautiful	Cedarville

Rock Hudson played the President of the United States in the mini-series *World War III* in 1982.

Daytime television talk show host **Oprah Winfrey** was the first African-American woman to anchor Nashville's WVTF-TV. She was nineteen years old.

Approximately 23 million people watch **The Oprah Winfrey Show** each week in the United States.

The television show **Bewitched** aired from 1964 to 1972. The show was set in the upscale community of Westport, Connecticut. Its main characters, the Stephenses, were husband Darrin (Dick York, later replaced by Dick Sargent) and his witch-wife Samantha (Elizabeth Montgomery), known for twitching her nose to get her way.

M*A*S*H, the television series, ran from 1972 to 1983. A less popular series was the spin-off entitled *After M*A*S*H*, which ran from 1983 to 1985. M.A.S.H. is the acronym for Mobile Army Surgical Hospital Unit.

Aaron Spelling's **Beverly Hills 90210** aired for 293 episodes.

40% of **Americans** watch television while they eat dinner.

The animated show **South Park** was created by Matt Stone and Trey Parker. First started on the internet, the show began airing in 1997 on cable channel Comedy Central.

MTV's first season of the reality show **The Real World** (1992) was filmed in New York City. The first seven participants picked to "Live in a house and have their lives taped, and find out what happens when people stop being polite and start getting real" were:

Andre Comeau (singer/songwriter)
Rebecca Blasband (singer/songwriter)
Eric Nies (model/actor)
Heather B. Gardner (hip-hop artist)
Julie Oliver (dancer)
Kevin Powell (journalist/activist)
Norman Korpi (visual artist)

Contestants of CBS's **Survivor** could be eliminated for breaking any of the following rules:

Entering the production area
Breaking the law
Missing an Island Council
Damaging the island environment

The **Miss America pageant** began in 1921. The pageant was first televised in 1954. It was first televised in color in 1966.

The first name of Mr. Rogers, of the children's show **Mister Rogers,** was Fred.

MOVIES

The 1986 film **Top Gun**, directed by Tony Scott, launched the careers of some leading celebrities including:

Tom Cruise as Lt. Pete "Maverick" Mitchell
Kelly McGillis as Charlotte "Charlie" Blackwood
Val Kilmer as Lt. Tom "Iceman" Kazanski
Anthony Edwards as Lt. Nick "Goose" Bradshaw
Tim Robbins as Lt. Sam "Merlin" Wells
Meg Ryan as Carole Bradshaw

ACTRESS TERI GARR HAS BEEN CREDITED IN FILMS AS:
Terry Carr
Terri Garr
Terry Garr
Teri Hope

Snow White and the Seven Dwarfs was Disney's first animated feature film. It premiered in 1937.

Ask your friends—most of them can't name the **Seven Dwarfs**:

Doc
Dopey
Sneezy
Happy
Sleepy
Bashful
Grumpy

The **Annual Saturn Awards** are handed out by the Academy of Science Fiction, Fantasy and Horror Films.

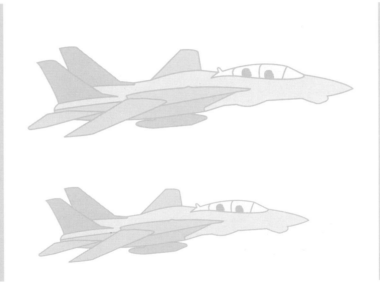

Director **Jim Jarmusch** made his first film, *Permanent Vacation,* in 1980 with a budget of approximately $15,000.

India produces more movies per year than the United States.

The real name of the film comedians, **the Marx Brothers**, were as follows:
Groucho: Julius
Harpo: Adolph
Chico: Leonard
Zeppo: Herbert

The fifth Marx brother, Gummo (Milton), was the only one who did not appear in any of the Marx Brothers' films.

The famous **Hollywood** sign in Los Angeles originally read "Hollywoodland."

In 1929, there were 20,000 **movie theaters** in the United States.

The **first drive-in movie theater** in America opened in Camden, New Jersey in 1933. Admission was twenty cents for each person and twenty-five cents for the car.

The **first movie theater** in the United States opened in New Orleans in 1896. Admission was ten cents.

The top five movie songs of all time, as chosen by a poll of jurors from **The American Film Institute**, are (in order of popularity):

"Over the Rainbow" (*The Wizard of Oz*, 1939)
"As Time Goes By" (*Casablanca*, 1942)
"Singin' in the Rain" (*Singin' in the Rain*, 1952)
"Moon River" (*Breakfast at Tiffany's*, 1961)
"White Christmas" (*Holiday Inn*, 1942)

The films that won the **Best Picture Oscar** for the 1980s were:

1980 *Ordinary People*
1981 *Chariots of Fire*
1982 *Gandhi*
1983 *Terms of Endearment*
1984 *Amadeus*
1985 *Out of Africa*
1986 *Platoon*
1987 *The Last Emperor*
1988 *Rain Man*
1989 *Driving Miss Daisy*

Director Peter Bogdanovich's 1971 film, **The Last Picture Show,** has been preserved in the U.S. National Film Registry.

Stanley Kubrick's film, **Dr. Strangelove,** premiered in January 1964, the year after President Kennedy signed the Limited Test Ban Treaty prohibiting nuclear testing in the atmosphere.

John F. Kennedy assassination witness Jean Hill consulted for Oliver Stone's 1991 film, **JFK**.

The Graduate, starring Dustin Hoffman, was based on the Charles Webb novel of the same name. **The Godfather**, starring Marlon Brando, was based on the Mario Puzo novel of the same name.

The original **Star Wars** was released in May 1977.

Cary Grant never won an Oscar.

You may recognize **Norma Jean Baker** as the real name of **Marilyn Monroe**, but what about:
Roy Fitzgerald (Rock Hudson)
Frederick Austerlitz (Fred Astaire)
Marion Michael Morrison (John Wayne)
Allen Stewart Konigsberg (Woody Allen)
Archie Leach (Cary Grant)

Some might not recognize **Getting Even** and **Without Feathers** as Woody Allen titles. They're collections of his short stories.

The name of the angel in Frank Capra's Christmas classic, **It's a Wonderful Life**, is Clarence. He was played by Henry Travers.

Almost Famous is director Cameron Crowe's semi-autobiographical film about going on the road with the Allman Brothers Band.

The first sound-on-film motion picture was **Phonofilm**. It was shown at the Rivoli Theater in New York City in April, 1923.

The budget for makeup in the 1968 film **Planet of the Apes** was $1 million.

TOP-TEN ALL-TIME VHS RENTALS:

Pretty Woman
Top Gun
The Little Mermaid
Home Alone
Ghost
The Lion King
Beauty and the Beast
Terminator 2: Judgment Day
Forrest Gump
Aladdin

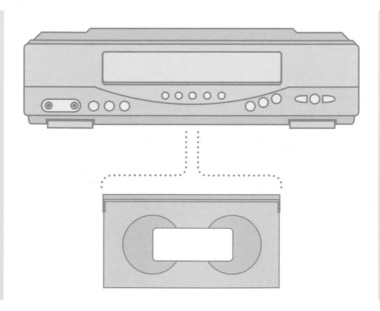

ANIMALS

TOP-TEN FASTEST LAND ANIMALS

Cheetah	70 mph
Pronghorn Antelope	61 mph
Wildebeest	50 mph
Lion	50 mph
Thomson's Gazelle	50 mph
Quarter Horse	47.5 mph
Elk	45 mph
Cape Hunting Dog	45 mph
Coyote	43 mph
Gray Fox	42 mph

The **marmoset** is one of the smallest monkeys in the world, weighing approximately 10 to 12 ounces.

A **giraffe's** neck can be over 5 feet in length.

The top 10 dog breeds registered with the **American Kennel Club**:

Labrador Retriever
Golden Retriever
German Shepherd
Dachshund
Beagle
Yorkshire Terrier
Poodle
Boxer
Chihuahua
Shih Tzu

Talcum powder kills ants.

MARMOSET

Social groups: family groups of up to 30 individuals (in captivity max 12). Only one breeding pair in a group.

Lifespan: 7-20 years

Length: Head & Body: 7-12 inches (18-30 cm)

Tail: 7-16 inches (17-40 cm)

Each **polar bear** in the arctic will walk approximately 100,000 miles in its lifetime.

It takes over 5,000 **silkworms** to produce 2 pounds of silk.

A **Tasmanian devil** is a marsupial.

Lions sleep an average of 20 hours per day.

Endangered animals in the United States include the **red fox**, the **humpback whale**, and the **gray bat**.

Humans have the longest lifespan of all mammals.

Most **fish** do not sleep.

Norway lemmings can breed when they are two weeks old.

The **Asian elephant** has the longest tail of all mammals. It is approximately 59 inches long.

Bee hummingbirds lay the smallest eggs of birds.

Webbed feet help **birds** to swim and to keep them from sinking into mud.

The longest snake is the **reticulated python**—it can grow to a length of 35 feet.

Bees can travel at a speed of up to 15 miles per hour.

There are roughly 47 billion **chickens** in the world.

A **kangaroo's** jump can be over 30 feet long and 10 feet high.

John Muir founded the **Sierra Club** in 1892.

The first zoo in the United States, the **Philadelphia Zoological Gardens**, opened in 1874.

A **skunk** can shoot its scented body oil a distance of 8-10 feet.

A worldwide **ban on whaling** began in 1986.

Angora wool comes from **rabbits**.

Wire-haired Fox Terriers see in color.

Cats cannot taste sweetness.

Milk gives cats diarrhea.

Studies show that **butterflies** follow actual flight patterns.

Tarantulas are the largest spiders in the world.

The **bison** is the official state animal of three U.S. states: Kansas, Oklahoma, and Wyoming.

The state bird of New Jersey is the **Eastern Goldfinch**.

Hogs have 34 to 44 teeth.

An **elephant's** tusks are actually teeth.

Praying mantises are known for cannibalistic behavior. The female praying mantis bites the head off her partner after they mate.

The slowest mammal is the **sloth**.

Ostriches, emus, and penguins are all **birds that can't fly**.

Chow Chow dogs have blue tongues.

10 of the 37 Registered Cat Breeds are:
Persian
Maine Coon
Exotic
Siamese
Abyssinian
Birman
Oriental
American Shorthair
Tonkinese
Burmese

Dogs cannot sweat; they have to pant to cool down.

All **horses** are given the same birthday: January 1.

Ten thousand people attended the **Grand Show of Domestic Poultry and Convention of Fowl Breeders**, an event that took place in Boston in 1849.

Every **giraffe** has a different pattern of spots.

Ferrets sleep about 16 hours a day.

A baby eagle is called an **eaglet**.

The gestation period of a **rabbit** is about 31 days.

Cats are the **most popular pets** in the United States, beating out dogs.

A **cat's sense of smell** is fourteen times more acute than that of a human.

The **Great Dane** is the tallest breed of dog.

The **chihuahua** is the smallest breed of dog in the world.

■ **Seals** can stay under water for up to 30 minutes.

■ There are over 2,500 different types of **snakes** in the world. Approximately 400 are poisonous.

■ **Bison** are born orange.

■ The **wolverine** is the largest member of the weasel family.

■ The pig-like noise pugs make is known as a **chortle**.

■ **Saltwater crocodiles** can weigh up to one ton.

■ A mother **lemur** will carry her baby in her mouth until the newborn can hang on to her fur on its own.

■ **Elephants** are the largest land mammals.

■ An adult **orangutan's** arm span is double its height.

■ The national symbol for the United States is the **North American Bald Eagle**.

■ The **manatee** is an endangered species; there are only 3,000 left in the U.S.

■ A **giant panda** cub weighs about 4 ounces at birth. As an adult it can weigh up to almost 300 pounds.

■ **Dolphins** must surface every two minutes to inhale oxygen through their blowholes.

■ **John James Audubon** proved that migratory birds return to the place where they were hatched.

POLITICS

So your presidential candidate-of-choice won South Dakota, Vermont, Wyoming, Montana, Maine, Nebraska, and Nevada and didn't come close to winning the election? Here's why:

ELECTORAL VOTES PER STATE

Alabama	9
Alaska	3
Arizona	10
Arkansas	6
California	55
Colorado	9
Connecticut	7
Delaware	3
District of Columbia	3
Florida	27
Georgia	15
Hawaii	4
Idaho	4
Illinois	21
Indiana	11
Iowa	7
Kansas	6
Kentucky	8
Louisiana	9
Maine	4
Maryland	10
Massachusetts	12
Michigan	17
Minnesota	10
Mississippi	6
Missouri	11
Montana	3
Nebraska	5

Nevada	5
New Hampshire	4
New Jersey	15
New Mexico	5
New York	31
North Carolina	15
North Dakota	3
Ohio	20
Oklahoma	7
Oregon	7
Pennsylvania	21
Rhode Island	4
South Carolina	8
South Dakota	3
Tennessee	11
Texas	34
Utah	5
Vermont	3
Virginia	13
Washington	11
West Virginia	5
Wisconsin	10
Wyoming	3

The first female presidential candidate was **Victoria Clafin Woodhull**. She was nominated in 1872 by the **Equal Rights Party**.

Jeannette Rankin was the **first female member of Congress**. She was elected to the House of Representatives (as a Republican) in 1916.

The first women's suffrage law giving **women the right to vote** in the United States was passed in Wyoming on December 10, 1869.

A total of eight **United States presidents were born in Virginia**—more than in any other state.

Golda Meir served as the **Prime Minister of Israel** from 1969 to 1974.

Mikhail Gorbachev was the last president of the Soviet Union.

The **Marshall Plan**, the program through which the United States gave economic aid to European countries to rebuild after World War II, was named after then Secretary of State, George C. Marshall.

D-Day, the Allied invasion of German-occupied France during World War II, occurred on June 6, 1944.

OPEC (The Organization of Petroleum Exporting Countries) was founded in 1960 to unify policies and regulate prices for the exportation of crude oil to other parts of the world. The original member countries were:

Iran
Iraq
Kuwait
Saudi Arabia
Venezuela

Jackson, Mississippi; Madison, Wisconsin; Lincoln, Nebraska; and Jefferson City, Missouri are all **state capitals named after United States presidents**.

The **Outer Space Treaty**, prohibiting the use of nuclear weapons in space, took effect on October 10, 1967.

William Henry Harrison had the shortest term in office of any President of the United States. He died thirty-one days after his inauguration.

Henry VI was less than a year old when he became the king of England in 1422.

Buckingham Palace in London was built in 1703 by the Duke of Buckingham.

Queen Victoria (UK) is the longest reigning queen (1837-1901) in history.

Janet Reno was the first female Attorney General. She was sworn into office in 1993.

The **Roe v. Wade** decision, which granted women the legal right to abortion, was rendered by the Supreme Court on January 22, 1973.

Carl B. Stokes, the first black mayor elected in America, served as the mayor of Cleveland, Ohio from 1967 to 1971.

The presidents whose faces are carved on **Mount Rushmore** are George Washington, Thomas Jefferson, Abraham Lincoln, and Theodore Roosevelt.

Napoleon Bonaparte crowned himself emperor of France in 1804.

President Theodore Roosevelt won the Nobel Peace Prize in 1906 for his efforts in bringing Russia and Japan together to create a treaty that ended the Russo-Japanese War (1904-1905).

World War I was fought from 1914 to 1918. America did not enter the war until 1917.

The **Berlin Wall** separated East Berlin and West Berlin from 1961 to 1989.

World War II was fought from 1939 to 1945.

The Pentagon building in Virginia really has five sides. It is the headquarters for the United States Department of Defense.

The **donkey** is the symbol of the Democratic party. The **elephant** is the symbol of the Republican party. Both symbols were introduced by Thomas Nast in political cartoons in 1874.

The three branches of the **Federal Government** are:

Legislative
Executive
Judicial

Blue laws in the United States prohibit the opening of some businesses and selling of items such as alcohol on Sundays.

The first ten amendments to the Constitution are known as the **Bill of Rights**.

The **President of the United States** can veto federal bills.

Sandra Day O'Connor was the first woman to serve on the Supreme Court. She was appointed by President Ronald Reagan in 1981.

President **John F. Kennedy** was assassinated by Lee Harvey Oswald in Dallas, Texas on November 22, 1963.

U.S. Presidents

NAME	FIRST YEAR OF OFFICE
George Washington	1789
John Adams	1797
Thomas Jefferson	1801
James Madison	1809
James Monroe	1817
John Quincy Adams	1825
Andrew Jackson	1829
Martin Van Buren	1837
William Henry Harrison	1841
John Tyler	1841
James Knox Polk	1845
Zachary Taylor	1849
Millard Fillmore	1850
Franklin Pierce	1853
James Buchanan	1857
Abraham Lincoln	1861
Andrew Johnson	1865
Ulysses Simpson Grant	1869
Rutherford Birchard Hayes	1877
James Abram Garfield	1881
Chester Alan Arthur	1881
(Stephen) Grover Cleveland	1885
Benjamin Harrison	1889
(Stephen) Grover Cleveland	1893
William McKinley	1897
Theodore Roosevelt	1901
William Howard Taft	1909
(Thomas) Woodrow Wilson	1913
Warren Gamaliel Harding	1921
(John) Calvin Coolidge, Jr.	1923
Herbert Clark Hoover	1929
Franklin Delano Roosevelt	1933
Harry S Truman	1945
Dwight David Eisenhower	1953

U.S. Presidents (continued)

NAME	FIRST YEAR OF OFFICE
John Fitzgerald Kennedy	1961
Lyndon Baines Johnson	1963
Richard Milhous Nixon	1969
Gerald Rudolph Ford, Jr.	1974
James Earl Carter	1977
Ronald Wilson Reagan	1981
George Herbert Walker Bush	1989
William Jefferson Clinton	1993
George Walker Bush	2001

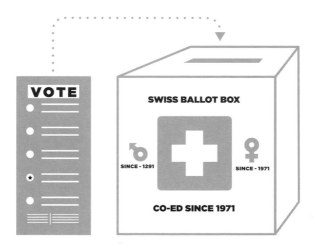

VOTE

SWISS BALLOT BOX

SINCE - 1291

SINCE - 1971

CO-ED SINCE 1971

Jimmy Carter, the 39th President of the United States, was once a peanut farmer.

John Quincy Adams was the first president's son to become president.

Fidel Castro took control of Cuba in 1959.

Although **Ronald Reagan** is known for having been an actor before going into politics, he was also a radio sports announcer.

Calvin Coolidge is the only United States President who had the same birthday as the nation: July 4.

Thomas Jefferson and **John Adams** both died on July 4, 1826, the fiftieth anniversary of the signing of the Declaration of Independence.

George Washington had to borrow money to get from Mount Vernon to New York City for his inauguration.

Thurgood Marshall was the first African-American appointed to the Supreme Court. He served from 1967 to 1991.

The **American Whig Party** was a political party formed in the 1834 to oppose Andrew Jackson and the Democrats. United States Presidents William Henry Harrison, John Tyler, Zachary Taylor, and Millard Fillmore were Whigs.

Switzerland was the last western country to give women the right to vote. The year was 1971.

Grover Cleveland was the only president to serve two nonconsecutive terms: 1885-1889 and 1893-1897.

President Rutherford B. Hayes banished liquor from the White House during his term of office.

U.S. Presidents named **James**:
James Madison, 4th President
James Monroe, 5th President
James Knox Polk, 11th President
James Buchanan, 15th President
James Abram Garfield, 20th President
James (Jimmy) Earl Carter, 39th President

In a speech to Congress on January 6, 1941, **President Franklin Delano Roosevelt** named **Four Freedoms** as essential: freedom of speech, freedom of religion, freedom from want, and freedom from fear.

President Harry S Truman was the first president to speak from the White House on television. The year was 1947.

Woodrow Wilson was the first American president to cross the Atlantic after he was elected.

Medicare began in July 1966.

NATO stands for the North Atlantic Treaty Organization, established in 1949.

President Bill Clinton's impeachment trial lasted from January 7 to February 12, 1999.

In the United States, **candidates for the presidency** must be born in the U.S. and be at least 35 years old.

The Supreme Court justices voted 5 to 4 in *Bush v. Gore*, ruling that the election recounts for the **2000 Presidential Election** should cease.

Ronald Reagan was the oldest president to take office. He was 69. The youngest presidents were **John F. Kennedy** and **Bill Clinton**, who both took office at the age of 46.

Woodrow Wilson was the only president with a Ph.D. He held a doctorate of political science from Johns Hopkins University.

Ronald Reagan carried every state in the 1984 presidential election against Walter Mondale except for Minnesota and the District of Columbia.

The first political party in the United States was the **Federalist Party,** which formed in 1789.

Jane Byrne became the first female mayor of Chicago in 1979.

WEATHER

CITIES THAT GET MORE ANNUAL RAINFALL THAN SEATTLE:

Chicago
Houston
New York City
Miami

Hurricanes are measured on the Saffir-Simpson Scale. Here are the categories:

CATEGORY	WIND SPEED	STORM SURGE	SEVERITY
1	74-95 mph	4-5 feet	Weak
2	96-110 mph	6-8 feet	Moderate
3	111-130 mph	9-12 feet	Strong
4	131-155 mph	13-18 feet	Very strong
5	above 155 mph	above 18 feet	Devastating

The first **umbrella factory** was established in Baltimore, Maryland in 1828.

Each year, hurricanes are named in **alphabetical order**; the first hurricane of the year starts with the letter "A."

A **moonbow** is a rainbow that takes place at night. It is also known as a lunar rainbow.

A hailstorm that fell on **Dallas** and **Forth Worth, Texas** in May 1995 caused $2 billion in damages.

The **highest U.S. temperature on record** is 134° (Fahrenheit), recorded in Death Valley, California, on July 10, 1913.

A powerful **earthquake** may release 10,000 times more energy than that of the first atomic bomb.

The **deadliest tornado** on record occurred in three states (Missouri, Illinois, and Indiana) on March 18, 1925, killing 689 people.

The **Farmer's Almanac** lists various information, including information on the best days to castrate animals, quit smoking, and make jams and jellies.

Wind speed is measured in knots.

Great Falls, Montana averages the highest wind speed in the United States.

The **Mojave Desert** in California has been known to go without rainfall for two years.

Shooting stars aren't really stars, but meteors that burn up in the earth's atmosphere.

There are ten **types of clouds**:

Cirrus
Cirrocumulus
Cirrostratus
Altocumulus
Altostratus
Nimbostratus
Stratocumulus
Stratus
Cumulus
Cumulonimbus

The **eye** of the hurricane is the center of the storm. It is usually calm.

Snow fell for 36 straight hours in New York in 1888. The storm, which dropped up to 50 inches of snow, became known as the **Great Blizzard of '88.**

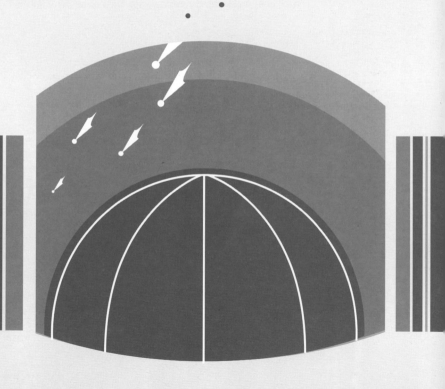

ART

The mysterious **Unicorn Tapestries** (dated from the late fifteenth and early sixteenth centuries) are on permanent display at the medieval branch of the Metropolitan Museum of Art, known as the Cloisters, in New York City.

Artist **Robert Smithson**, known for his massive outdoor piece entitled *Spiral Jetty,* died in a plane crash in Amarillo, Texas in 1973 at the age of 35. In 2005, in association with the Whitney Museum of American Art, his drawing for a park to be pulled by a tugboat around the Island of Manhattan came to life in a piece entitled *Floating Island*.

Famed American painter **Norman Rockwell** became the art director of *Boy's Life* magazine while he was still a teenager.

Renowned artist **Keith Haring** opened a retail store in Soho in Manhattan, called the Pop Shop, so that people would have access to his designs on items such as T-shirts and buttons at a low cost.

Before he decided to become an artist, **Vincent van Gogh** worked as an evangelist in Belgium.

Painter **Paul Gauguin** was once a stockbroker.

The **National Endowment for the Arts** was founded in 1965. Since its creation, this public agency has awarded over 120,000 grants to support the arts.

Andy Warhol's famous Factory hangout in New York City was originally located at 221 East 47th Street.

FAMOUS MUSEUMS AND THEIR LOCATIONS:

Louvre	Paris, France
Metropolitan Museum of Art	New York, U.S.A.
Museum of Modern Art	New York, U.S.A.
Solomon R. Guggenheim Museum	New York, U.S.A.
Smithsonian Institute	Washington, D.C., U.S.A.
Tate Gallery	London, England
Uffizi Gallery	Florence, Italy
Van Gogh Museum	Amsterdam, Netherlands
British Museum	London, England

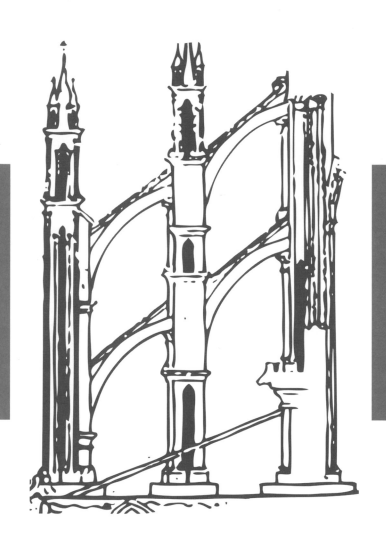

■ Charles M. Schulz's comic strip **Peanuts** debuted in October, 1950.

American Gothic, the famous painting of a couple with a pitchfork, was done by Grant Wood in 1930. The couple that posed for the painting were his dentist and his sister.

■ Doric, Ionic, and Corinthian are the three main styles of **Greek architecture**.

■ A **flying buttress** is an arched support for the exterior wall of a building.

■ The leading ballerina of a dance company is called the **prima ballerina**.

■ The ballet **Swan Lake** was written by Peter Ilyich Tchaikovsky.

The **Hall of Mirrors** in the Palace of Versailles was commissioned by King Louis XIV of France in the seventeenth century.

Leonardo da Vinci's fresco, **The Last Supper**, is in the Church of Santa Maria delle Grazie in Milan, Italy.

The deep red sunset seen in Norwegian Edvard Munch's **The Scream** is believed to reflect the intense sunsets seen throughout the world following the 1883 eruption of the Indonesian volcano Krakatoa.

■ The earliest form of **ballet** has been traced back to the 1400s.

■ The real name of the painter **El Greco** was Doménikos Theotokópoulos.

The comic strip **"Little Orphan Annie"** appeared for the first time in the *New York Daily News* on August 5, 1925.

■ **The National Gallery of Art** opened in Washington, D.C. on March 17, 1941.

SCIENCE

■ The only woman to win two Nobel prizes is **Marie Curie** (1903, 1911).

■ Scientist **Albert Einstein** played the violin.

■ The **sun** has a volume 1,300,000 times that of Earth's.

■ The **Mars Pathfinder** spacecraft returned 16,500 images from its 3-month period of transmitting data and pictures in 1997.

■ There are more than 60 species of **sunflowers**.

■ The **speed of sound** going through air is 1,116 feet per second. The speed of sound going through steel is 17,100 feet per second.

■ **Nuclear power plants** are responsible for generating 20% of the electric power in the United States.

■ **Earth Day** is April 22. It was established in the U.S. in 1969.

■ **NASA** selected the first female astronauts in January 1978.

■ The **orbital velocity of the earth** is 18.51 miles/second.

■ **Arbor Day** was founded by J. Sterling Morton in Nebraska City, Nebraska in 1872.

■ There are approximately 50,000,000,000 **galaxies** in the cosmos.

The **moon's cycle** is 27.3 days. The eight phases of the moon are:

New moon
Waning crescent
Last quarter
Waning gibbous
Full moon
Waxing gibbous
First quarter
Waxing crescent

The **first four planets** of our solar system, as they extend from the sun, are Mercury, Venus, Earth, and Mars. They are known as terrestrial planets. Earth is the largest terrestrial planet.

Aristarchus of Samos was the first astronomer to propose that the earth moves around the sun. Nicolaus Copernicus made the same argument in the sixteenth century—eighteen centuries after Aristarchus.

Earth's **atmosphere** is comprised of:
78% nitrogen
21% oxygen
1% argon, water, and trace gases

More than 70% of the surface of the Earth is covered with **water**.

Do Ursa Major and Ursa Minor sound familiar? They're the constellations better known as the **Big Dipper** and the **Little Dipper**.

"The Big Bang" theory holds that the universe was created 14 billion years ago when it expanded rapidly from a hot and dense state.

The surface of the earth is made up of 16 **tectonic plates**.

■ Scientists divide **living organisms** by kingdom, followed by phylum, class, order, family, genus, and species.

■ **Acid rain** doesn't just refer to rain. It's precipitation of any kind, including rain, snow, and fog, with high levels of sulfuric or nitric acid.

■ The **vernal equinox** marks the first day of spring. The **autumnal equinox** marks the beginning of fall. Summer begins on the day with the most sunlight of the year, known as the **summer solstice**. The **winter solstice** falls on the day with the shortest interval of sunlight.

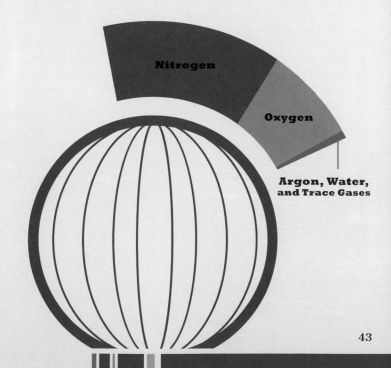

Nitrogen

Oxygen

Argon, Water, and Trace Gases

There are 88 identified **constellations**:

Andromeda	Cygnus	Pavo
Antila	Delphinus	Pegasus
Apus	Dorado	Perseus
Aquarius	Draco	Phoenix
Aquila	Equuleus	Pictor
Ara	Eridanus	Pisces
Aries	Foranx	Piscis Austrinus
Auriga	Gemini	Puppis
Boötes	Grus	Pyxis
Caelum	Hercules	Reticulum
Camelopardalis	Horologium	Sagitta
Cancer	Hydra	Sagittarius
Canes Venatici	Hydrus	Scorpio
Canis Major	Indus	Sculptor
Canis Minor	Lacerta	Scutum
Capricorn	Leo	Serpens
Carina	Leo Minor	Sextans
Cassiopeia	Lepus	Taurus
Centaurus	Libra	Telescopium
Cepheus	Lupus	Triangulum
Cetus	Lynx	Triangulum Australe
Chamaeleon	Lyra	Tucana
Circinus	Mensa	Ursa Major
Columbia	Microscopium	Ursa Minor
Coma Berencies	Monoceros	Vela
Corona Austrina	Musca	Virgo
Corona Borealis	Norma	Volans
Corvus	Octans	Vulpecula
Crater	Ophiuchus	
Crux	Orion	

■ **Halley's Comet** returns to Earth every 76 years.

■ The **Atlantic Ocean** gets wider by several inches every year.

┃ The first successfully cloned mammal was a sheep named **Dolly**. She was born in 1996 in Scotland. Ian Wilmut is credited with the cloning.

┃ **Charles Darwin** explained his theory of evolution in *The Origin of Species*, published in 1859.

┃ The **asteroid belt** in Earth's solar system is found between the orbits of Mars and Jupiter.

■ Scientists believe the **earth** was formed 4.6 billion years ago.

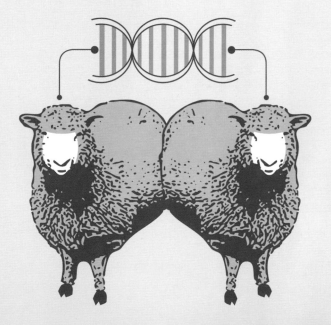

EDUCATION

The second oldest college in the U.S. is the **College of William and Mary** in Williamsburg, Virginia. The oldest is **Harvard University** in Cambridge, Massachusetts.

Test takers of the **College Board's SAT** test have 3 hours and 45 minutes to complete the exam.

U.S. Presidents who attended **Harvard University**:

John Adams
John Quincy Adams
Rutherford B. Hayes
Theodore Roosevelt
Franklin D. Roosevelt
John F. Kennedy
George W. Bush

U.S. Presidents who attended **Yale University**:

Gerald Ford
George H.W. Bush
George W. Bush
Bill Clinton

The first female Greek-letter society was **Kappa Alpha Theta** in 1870 at DePauw University in Greencastle, Indiana.

There are approximately one billion **illiterate adults** in the world.

The life expectancy of **American high school dropouts** is 9.2 years less than that of graduates.

Literary mega-star **Dave Eggers** (*A Heartbreaking Work of Staggering Genius*) founded the writing/tutoring center 826 Valencia Street, in San Francisco, California.

Musician **Billy Joel**, singer **Wayne Newton,** and actor **Cary Grant** were all high-school dropouts.

In 1999, **Jones University** became the first online university to be fully accredited by the Higher Learning Commission.

The **first circulating library** was founded by Benjamin Franklin in Philadelphia in 1731.

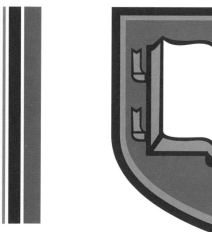

THE IVY LEAGUE

Harvard	Cambridge, MA
Yale	New Haven, CT
Princeton	Princeton, NJ
Columbia	New York, NY
Brown	Providence, RI
Dartmouth	Hanover, NH
Cornell	Ithaca, NY
University of Pennsylvania	Philadelphia, PA

THE SEVEN SISTERS

Barnard College	New York, NY
Bryn Mawr College	Bryn Mawr, PA
Mount Holyoke College	South Hadley, MA
Radcliffe College	Cambridge, MA
Smith College	Northampton, MA
Vassar College	Poughkeepsie, NY
Wellesley College	Wellesley, MA

The most popular country for U.S. students to study abroad in is the **United Kingdom**.

The first Fine Arts Department in a U.S. College was the **School of Fine Arts at Yale University** (New Haven, Connecticut), founded in 1864.

The first arts department to award degrees in the field of art was the **College of Fine Arts at Syracuse University** (Syracuse, New York), founded in 1873.

Montessori schools are based on the ideas of twentieth-century Italian educator Maria Montessori.

There are actually eleven schools in **"The Big Ten"**—Pennsylvania State University joined the original ten schools in the conference in 1990—and all but one are state universities:

University of Illinois (at Urbana-Champaign)
University of Iowa
University of Michigan
University of Minnesota
University of Wisconsin (at Madison)
Michigan State University
Ohio State University
Indiana University
Purdue University
Pennsylvania State University
*Northwestern University

*A private university

In 1838, **Oberlin College** became the first U.S. institution of higher learning to admit women.

West Point opened in New York State on July 4, 1802.

In 1962, **James H. Meredith** became the first African American admitted to the University of Mississippi.

FOOD & DRINK

■ The first **Jelly Belly**® flavors were root beer, grape, very cherry, lemon, cream soda, green apple, tangerine, and licorice.

■ **Maraschino cherries** are preserved cherries. Although they have the same name as the liquer maraschino, which they were sometimes preserved in, there is no liquer in the modern maraschino cherry.

■ The famed **Culinary Institute of America** (CIA) in Hyde Park, New York has a west coast location in St. Helena, California, called The Culinary Institute of America at Greystone.

■ **Wonder**® **Bread** became a national brand in 1925.

■ 500 million **Hostess**® **Twinkies** are sold every year. President Bill Clinton put one in a time capsule.

■ **Manhattan clam chowder** is red. **New England clam chowder** is white.

■ **Coca-Cola**® was first bottled in 1894 in Vicksburg, Mississippi.

■ In America, **Coca-Cola**® outsells **Pepsi**®. In Saudi Arabia and Quebec, the opposite is true.

■ **Krispy Kreme Doughnuts**® were first sold in July 1937.

■ About **one-fifth of all the wheat grown** in the United States comes from Kansas. That's why the state is called "The Breadbasket of the World."

■ In 1975, movie-man Francis Ford Coppola and his wife Eleanor purchased over 1,500 acres of land in California wine country and created the **Niebaum-Coppola Estate winery**.

■ A 12 oz.-cup of brewed **coffee** contains 200 mg of caffeine.

■ **Starbucks Coffee**®, founded in Pike Place Market in Seattle in 1971, has shops in 35 countries (including the United States).

■ A grande (16 oz.) **Mocha Frappuccino** blended coffee from Starbucks has 420 calories and 16 grams of fat.

■ The average ear of **corn** has 800 kernels.

■ A medium-sized **potato** provides 45% of the recommended daily value of vitamin C for an adult.

■ **Corn Flakes**® were invented in 1894 by brothers Will Keith Kellogg and Dr. John Harvey Kellogg.

■ The **first hot dog stand** in the world opened in St. Louis, Missouri in 1883.

■ **M&Ms**® were named after candy developers Forrest Mars, Sr. and Bruce Murrie.

■ **M&Ms**® **candies** were first made in 1941.

■ Artificial sweeteners **Dulcin and Cyclamate** were banned in the United States in 1954 and 1969, respectively.

■ **Nescafé**® was the first instant coffee. It was introduced in Europe in 1938.

■ **Peanuts** are legumes.

■ **Cream cheese** was invented in 1872. **Bagels** can be traced back to 1683.

■ Chinese restaurant item **chop suey** was invented in the U.S.

■ **Fulton, Kentucky** was once known as the "Banana Capital of the World" because 70% of imported bananas to the U.S. used to be shipped there.

■ The U.S. military has created an **"indestructible sandwich"** that can stay "fresh" for up to three years

■ A **lemon tree** can produce 500-600 pounds of fruit a year.

■ Some **nuts** are seeds or parts of seeds.

■ **Black olives** contain 10-30% more oil than green olives.

■ Whole **milk** contains at least 3.25% milk fat. Skim milk contains 0.5%.

■ The first patent for a **gelatin dessert** was obtained by Peter Cooper in 1845.

■ Kalamazoo, Michigan is known as **Celery City**.

■ **Wheat** has been cultivated on every continent except Antarctica.

■ The Aztecs considered **avocados** aphrodisiacs.

❚ California grows approximately 80% of all the **asparagus** in the United States.

❚ The red and white colors of the **Campbell's® Soup** label came from the colors of the Cornell University football team, which Campbell's executive Herberton Williams watched play in 1898.

■ **Bean curd** and **tofu** are the same thing.

❚ The most popular flavor of **ice cream** is vanilla, followed by chocolate, then butter pecan. Strawberry ranks fourth.

■ **Bacon** is made from the underside of a hog, also known as the pork belly.

■ **White** and **brown eggs** contain the same nutrients in the same quantities.

■ There are over 150 varieties of **potatoes**.

■ **Bananas** are comprised of 75% water.

❚ Diners who like to eat horizontally can enjoy homemade beef carpaccio in bed at **B.E.D.**, a restaurant with mattress seating in Miami, Florida.

■ A **jackfruit**, which is indigenous to India, can weigh about a hundred pounds.

❚ **Dom Perignon** (1638-1716), a Benedictine monk in France, is credited with developing the procedure for the production of champagne.

■ The base of **chewing gum** is made from chicle, which comes from sapodilla trees.

■ The common **sandwich** was named after John Montagu, fourth Earl of Sandwich (1718-1792), who invented it.

SANDWICH	MEAT INSIDE
Croque Monsieur	Ham
French Dip	Roast Beef
Reuben	Corned Beef
BLT	Bacon
PLT	Prosciutto

■ **Macadamia nuts** were named for John Macadam.

■ **Blood oranges** are also called Moro oranges.

■ **Venison** is deer meat.

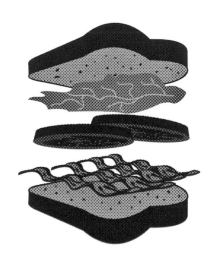

■ The Marquis de Sade loved **chocolate** and had it sent to him in prison.

■ The scientific name for the **tomato** is the *Lycopersicon esculentum.*

■ **Cotton candy** made its debut at the 1904 World's Fair in St. Louis.

▌ The first cooking school was started by **Juliet Carson** in New York City in 1876.

■ An **ice-cream-like concoction** could be found in 400 B.C. Persia.

■ The most popular **Ben & Jerry's**® ice cream flavor is Cherry Garcia.

■ Every **strawberry** has over 200 seeds on it.

■ **Eggplant** (also known as aubergine) can be either purple or white.

■ High-quality **cinnamon** comes from Sri Lanka.

▌ **Kellogg's Pop-Tarts**® come in 32 flavors including Chocolate Chip Cookie Dough, Frosted S'mores, Cinnamon, French Toast, Frosted Hot Fudge Sundae, and the old standby, Strawberry.

■ Post Cereals developed its first cereal, **Grape-Nuts**®, in 1897.

■ **Watermelon** is a vegetable.

■ The national drink of Iceland is a **potato schnapps** called "Black Death."

▌ Scotland's national dish, **haggis**, is made of minced heart, lungs, and trimmings of a lamb and oatmeal boiled in a sheep's stomach.

▌ **Scrod** is not the name of a specific fish. It refers to a young haddock, cod, or Alaskan pollock.

■ A **fig** is technically a flower.

The **fast food** name game:

Starbucks Coffee® Company was named after Starbuck, a character in Moby-Dick.

In Quebec Province, Canada, **Kentucky Fried Chicken**® (KFC) is named Poulet Frit Kentucky (PFK).

■ The state of Vermont produces the most **maple syrup** in the United States.

■ Most **grocery shopping** is done on Saturdays.

■ **Marzipan** (almond paste) is made of almonds and sugar.

■ The **hot dog** was invented by Charles Feltman in 1874.

To keep **guacamole** from turning brown, place the pit of an avocado in the bowl.

Hershey's® **Kisses** got their name because the machine that makes them looks like it's kissing the conveyor belt.

Beck's® is not only Germany's top export beer—it also accounts for 85% of all German beer exports to the United States.

In English pubs, ale is measured by pints and quarts. So in old England, when customers got unruly, the bartender used to yell at them to mind their own pints and quarts and settle down. From this we get the saying **"mind your Ps and Qs."**

■ There are over 5,900 **Dairy Queen's**® throughout the world.

■ There are over 3,000 varieties of **tea**.

■ **Budweiser** is the best-selling beer in the world.

GEOGRAPHY

■ The part of the U.S. that the sun shines on first is the top of **Mount Cadillac** in Maine.

■ The longest river in the world is the **Nile** in Egypt.

THE GREAT LAKES ARE:

Lake Superior
Lake Michigan
Lake Huron
Lake Erie
Lake Ontario

Longwood Gardens in Kennett Square, Pennsylvania, has over 1,000 acres of gardens and over 11,000 different types of plants. The gardens were created by Pierre S. du Pont and are visited by over 900,000 people each year.

The **U.S.S.R.** was made up of 15 Soviet Socialist Republics:

Armenia
Azerbaijan
Belorussia (now Belarus)
Estonia
Georgia
Kazakhstan
Kirgiziya (Kyrgyzstan)
Latvia
Lithuania
Moldavia (now Moldova)
Russia
Tajikistan
Turkmenistan
Ukraine
Uzbekistan

Least densely populated countries in the world (in descending order):

Mongolia
Nambia
Australia
Suriname
Botswana
Mauritania
Iceland
Libya
Guyana
Canada
Source: World Almanac

Smallest countries in the world by area (in descending order):

Vatican City
Monaco
Nauru
Tuvalu
San Marino
Liechtenstein
Marshall Islands
Maldives
Malta
Grenada, Saint Vincent, and the Grenadines
Source: World Almanac

Countries with the **largest populations** in the world
(in descending order)**:**

China
India
United States
Indonesia
Brazil
Russia
Pakistan
Japan
Bangladesh
Nigeria
Source: World Almanac

Largest countries in the world by area (in descending order)**:**

Russia
Canada
China
United States
Brazil
Australia
India
Argentina
Kazakhstan
Sudan
Source: World Almanac

The New York borough of **Queens** was named for the queen consort of
Charles II of England.

New York, Pennsylvania, New Jersey, Delaware, and Maryland are known
collectively as the **Mid-Atlantic states**.

New York City is comprised of five boroughs:

Manhattan
The Bronx
Brooklyn
Staten Island
Queens

The longest suspension bridge in the United States is the **Verrazano Narrows** in New York. It spans 4,260 feet.

The longest bridge span in the world is the **Akashi Kaikyo Bridge** in Japan. It spans 6,527 feet.

Stonehenge, in England, built on a site that dates to around 2800 B.C. The erected monoliths seem to be closer to 2400-2300 B.C.

The **Pyramids of Egypt** are said to have been built starting between 2600 and 2700 B.C.

The Spanish explorer **Juan Ponce de León** discovered Florida while searching for the Fountain of Youth.

The **Seven Wonders of the Ancient World** are:

The Colossus of Rhodes
The Hanging Gardens of Babylon
The Lighthouse of Alexandria
The Great Pyramid of Giza
The Statue of Zeus at Olympia
The Temple of Artemis at Ephesus
The Mausoleum at Helicarnassus

4.7 million people visit the **Grand Canyon** every year.

The **Taj Mahal** in Agra, India was built by Shan Jahan as a tomb for his wife. The structure was built between 1632 and 1650.

■ **Christmas Island** is in the eastern Indian Ocean.

■ The northernmost point in the United States is the city of **Point Barrow, Alaska**.

■ **Hawaii** is comprised of 132 islands.

STATE	CAPITAL
Alabama	Montgomery
Alaska	Juneau
Arizona	Phoenix
Arkansas	Little Rock
California	Sacramento
Colorado	Denver
Connecticut	Hartford
Delaware	Dover
Florida	Tallahassee
Georgia	Atlanta
Hawaii	Honolulu
Idaho	Boise
Illinois	Springfield
Indiana	Indianapolis
Iowa	Des Moines
Kansas	Topeka
Kentucky	Frankfort
Louisiana	Baton Rouge
Maine	Augusta
Maryland	Annapolis
Massachusetts	Boston
Michigan	Lansing
Minnesota	St. Paul
Mississippi	Jackson
Missouri	Jefferson City
Montana	Helena
Nebraska	Lincoln
Nevada	Carson City

New Hampshire	Concord
New Jersey	Trenton
New Mexico	Santa Fe
New York	Albany
North Carolina	Raleigh
North Dakota	Bismark
Ohio	Columbus
Oklahoma	Oklahoma City
Oregon	Salem
Pennsylvania	Harrisburg
Rhode Island	Providence
South Carolina	Columbia
South Dakota	Pierre
Tennessee	Nashville
Texas	Austin
Utah	Salt Lake City
Vermont	Montpelier
Virginia	Richmond
Washington	Olympia
West Virginia	Charlestown
Wisconsin	Madison
Wyoming	Cheyenne

The **United Kingdom** consists of:

England
Scotland
Wales
Northern Ireland

The native name for **Greenland** is Kalaallit Nunaat.

There is a city named **Kansas City** in both the states of Missouri and Kansas.

The highest uninterrupted waterfall in the world is **Angel Falls** in Venezuela.
It has a 3,212-foot drop.

Disneyland is in Anaheim, California. **Walt Disney World** is in Lake Buena Vista, Florida.

There is a Danish village named **"A"** and a French village named **"Y."**

Beijing, China, was formerly known as Beiping.

An **archipelago** is a group of islands.

Loch Ness is a lake in Scotland. The legendary Loch Ness monster is said to live there.

The **San Andreas Fault** extends for more than 800 miles from Mexico to a point north of San Francisco in California.

The **Mason-Dixon** line runs between Pennsylvania and Maryland. It is often considered the dividing point between the northern and southern states.

Motor City and Motown are nicknames for **Detroit**, Michigan because the city is the center for car production in the United States.

The **Thames** is the longest river in England.

Denver, Colorado is often called the "Mile-High City" because it stands at an altitude of over 5,000 feet, just under one mile.

There are more national parks in **southern Utah** than any other place in the United States.

Latitude is the measurement of degrees of distance north or south of the Equator.

Longitude is the measurement of degrees east or west of the prime meridian, which runs through Greenwich, England.

Timbuktu is a city in Mali in western Africa.

■ Half of the earth's surface is known as a **hemisphere**.

■ The southernmost tip of Africa is **Cape of Agulhas**.

■ The **Pacific Ocean** is the largest ocean in the world.

■ **Crete** is the largest of the Greek islands.

■ The lowest point of dry land on Earth is the shore of the **Dead Sea**, between Jordan and Israel, which is approximately 1,300 feet below sea level.

Size of Continents

PLACE	LAND AREA
Asia (and Middle East)	17,212,048 square miles
Africa	11,608,161 square miles
North America (and Central America and the Caribbean)	9,449,464 square miles
South America	6,879,954 square miles
Antarctica	5,100,023 square miles
Europe	3,837,083 square miles
Australia (and Oceania)	2,967,967 square miles

■ 25% of the state of **California** is made up of deserts.

■ The famous "strip" of **Las Vegas** is on Las Vegas Boulevard.

■ **Brazil** is the largest country in South America. With an area of approximately 3 million square miles, it takes up nearly 50% of the continent.

■ The **Erie Canal** (between Albany and Buffalo, New York) opened in 1825.

NATO (North Atlantic Treaty Organization) was established on August 24, 1949. The original members were:

United States of America
Canada
United Kingdom
France
Denmark
Iceland
Italy
Norway
Portugal
Belgium
Netherlands
Luxembourg

The **Sahara Desert** in North Africa has an area of 3,250,000 square miles.

FORMER NAMES OF COUNTRIES:

Iran	Persia
Sri Lanka	Ceylon
Taiwan	Formosa
Thailand	Siam
Zimbabwe	Rhodesia

NATIONAL MOTTOES:

Czech Republic: "Truth prevails!"
Jamaica: "Out of many, one people"
Kenya: "Let's work together"
Luxembourg: "We want to stay what we are"
Switzerland: "One for all, all for one"
Scotland: "No one injures me with impunity"

Kansas City, Missouri has more boulevards than Paris.

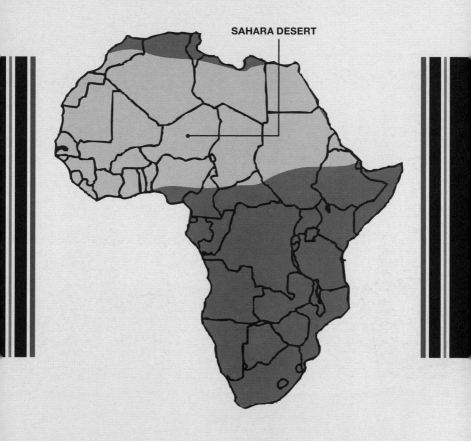

SAHARA DESERT

The country of **Spain** forms approximately five-sixths of the Iberian Peninsula.

The first U.S. commercial tea farm was established in **Summerville, South Carolina** in 1890.

Western **South Dakota** marks the geographic center of the United States, when Hawaii and Alaska are included.

Easter Island, a small island in the South Pacific, features large, mysterious, and striking statues (some weighing in at over 20 tons) of figures that some believe are depictions of Polynesian chiefs.

Kilimanjaro, the highest mountain in Africa, rises to a height of 19,431 feet.

At 6,288 feet high, **Mount Washington** in New Hampshire is the highest point in the northeastern United States.

The first officially designated national park in the world was **Yellowstone**. It opened in 1872.

Mount Blanc in the Alps is the highest point (15,780 feet) in France.

■ **The Grand Canyon** is 5,300 feet deep in some places.

■ **Piccadilly Circus** in London got its name from collars, called piccadills, that were made by a tailor (Robert Baker) who created them in the area.

■ Only 20 of the 3,000 coral islands and reefs that comprise the **Bahamas** are habitable.

■ The **Lincoln Tunnel** (which connects Manhattan and New Jersey) is the only three-tube underwater vehicular tunnel in the world.

WE ALL KNOW CALIFORNIA AS THE GOLDEN STATE, BUT DID YOU KNOW THESE STATE NAMES?

Louisiana	Pelican State
Maine	Pine Tree State
New Mexico	Land of Enchantment
Tennessee	Volunteer State
Utah	Beehive State

■ Visitors to **New York City** should remember that popular Houston Street is not pronounced like the well-known Texas city, but as "How-stin" Street.

■ The state with the most covered bridges is **Indiana.**

■ **West Virginia** was the first state to have a sales tax.

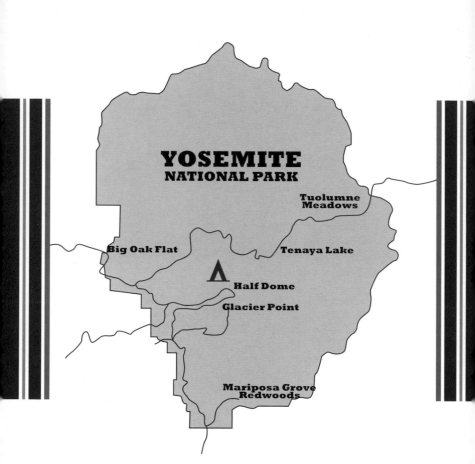

YOSEMITE
NATIONAL PARK

Tuolumne
Meadows

Big Oak Flat

Tenaya Lake

Half Dome

Glacier Point

Mariposa Grove
Redwoods

■ **San Jose** was the original capital of California.

■ **Manhattan** can be found in New York and Kansas.

■ **Gilroy, California** is the self-proclaimed "Garlic Capital of the World."

Yosemite National Park
John Muir helped convince Congress to declare California's **Yosemite** a National Park in 1890.
Yosemite gets **3.5 million visitors per year**.
Yosemite has **800 miles of hiking trails**.

People who live in:
Lexington, Kentucky are known as Lexingtonians
Ann Arbor, Michigan are known as Ann Arborites
Syracuse, New York are known as Syracusians
Dallas, Texas are known as Dallasites
Markham, Illinois are known as Markham People

People who live in:
Montenegro are known as Montenegrins
San Marino are known as Sammarinese

TRANSPORTATION

JetBlue Airways®, which started flying in February of 2000, was the first U.S. airline to broadcast the Olympic Games live at every passenger seat.

The **cable cars** of San Francisco are the only moving national landmarks.

The New York **MTA subway system** carries 4.5 million riders per day.

The **first underground subway system** was in England in 1863. It was powered by steam.

Charles Lindbergh, who made the first solo flight across the Atlantic, had a fear of heights.

The **Union Pacific** and **Central Pacific Railroads** met at Promontory Point, Utah on May 10, 1869, completing the transcontinental railroad.

Franklin D. Roosevelt had the first presidential airplane, but John F. Kennedy's VC-137 was the first to be called **Air Force One**.

In the United States, the **first coast-to-coast trip** in an auto took 63½ days. The year was 1903.

The Hindenburg airship exploded on May 6, 1937 at Lakehurst (N.J.) Naval Air Station, killing 36 people. At 803.8 feet in length and 135.1 feet in diameter, the German passenger airship was the largest aircraft that has ever flown.

The first **Volkswagen® Beetle** was introduced in the United States in 1949.

London's **Heathrow Airport** opened in 1955.

In London, **taxi drivers** lower their windows so potential passengers can tell them their destination, before getting into the taxi.

AIRPORT CODES FOR THE TEN BUSIEST AIRPORTS IN THE WORLD:

ATL	Hartsfield-Jackson Atlanta International Airport	Atlanta, Georgia
ORD	O'Hare International Airport	Chicago, Illinois
LHR	Heathrow International Airport	London, England
HND	Tokyo International Airport	Tokyo, Japan
LAX	Los Angeles International Airport	Los Angeles, California
DFW	Dallas/Ft. Worth International Airport	Dallas, Texas
FRA	Frankfurt International Airport	Frankfurt, Germany
CDG	Charles de Gaulle Airport	Paris, France
AMS	Schipol Airport	Amsterdam, The Netherlands
DEN	Denver International Airport	Denver, Colorado

The **Lincoln Highway** (from New York to California) was the first coast-to-coast highway in the United States. It opened for travel in 1913.

The **first metered taxis** were used in Germany in 1897.

The **first mountain bikes** were made in the United States in 1979 by Charles Kelly and Gary Fisher.

The last **Model T Ford** was produced on May 26, 1927.

The **Orient Express**, which traveled from Paris to Constantinople, was introduced in 1883.

The **first electric traffic light** was installed in Cleveland, Ohio in 1914.

Japanese bullet trains started running in 1965.

The **first parking meter in the United States** was installed in 1935.

Carhenge, a replica of England's Stonehenge, was built out of 38 American cars in Alliance, Nebraska.

The **first speed-limit** law in the United States was established in Connecticut in 1901. The limit for cars in cities was 10 m.p.h.

CELEBRITIES

CELEBRITY ASTROLOGICAL SIGNS

Johnny Depp	Gemini
Brad Pitt	Sagittarius
Ashton Kutcher	Aquarius
Gwyneth Paltrow	Gemini
Justin Timberlake	Aquarius
Naomi Campbell	Gemini

Actor **Dustin Hoffman** once worked as a toy salesman at Macy's.

CHILDHOOD STAR ACTRESSES WHO WENT ON TO SUCCESSFUL FILM CAREERS, AND THEIR FIRST MOVIES:

ACTRESS	FIRST MOVIE
Brooke Shields	*Communion*
Jodi Foster	*Napoleon and Samantha*
Natalie Portman	*Léon*
Sarah Jessica Parker	*Somewhere Tomorrow*
Drew Barrymore	*Altered States*

Movie star **Steve Buscemi** worked as a fireman from 1980 to 1984.

Famous Mothers and Daughters:

Goldie Hawn and Kate Hudson
Blythe Danner and Gwyneth Paltrow
Judy Garland and Liza Minelli
Debbie Reynolds and Carrie Fisher
Vanessa Redgrave and Natasha Richardson
Ingrid Bergman and Isabella Rossellini

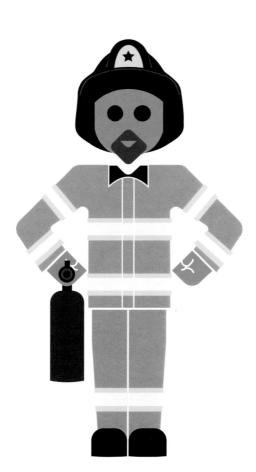

SCARY FILMS YOU MIGHT NOT ASSOCIATE WITH FUNNY MAN ROBIN WILLIAMS

Death to Smoochy
Insomnia
One Hour Photo
Dead Again

WHO'S TALL?

Clive Owen	6'2"
Keanu Reeves	6'1"
Uma Thurman	6'0"

WHO'S NOT?

Ben Stiller	5'8"
Tom Cruise	5'7"
Winona Ryder	5'4"
Helena Bonham Carter	5'3"

Mae West was born in Greenpoint, Brooklyn.

Actor **Clint Eastwood** worked pumping gas while he was a student on the G.I. Bill at Los Angeles City College.

Australian actress **Nicole Kidman** was born in Honolulu, Hawaii.

Actress **Gwyneth Paltrow** studied Art History at the University of California, Santa Barbara.

Actress **Angelina Jolie** is the goddaughter of Jacqueline Bisset.

Actor **Al Pacino** has never been married.

People magazine began its "Sexiest Man Alive" covers in 1985. The first honored: actor Mel Gibson.

- **Sarah Michelle Gellar** was once a competitive figure skater.

- **Lucille Ball** made her film debut in 1933. She and bandleader Desi Arnaz were married for 20 years before divorcing.

- **Brad Pitt** was born in Shawnee, Oklahoma.

- **Tom Cruise** attended a seminary to become a Catholic priest.

- Actor **Jack Nicholson** was born in Neptune, New Jersey.

- Actor **Nicolas Cage** is director Francis Ford Coppola's nephew.

- Actress **Diane Keaton** was a member of the original cast of the musical *Hair*.

- Actress **Natalie Portman** was discovered by a scout in a pizza parlor in 1991.

- Actresses **Bette Davis**, **Raquel Welch**, and **Lily Tomlin** all worked as waitresses at one time.

ELIZABETH TAYLOR'S HUSBANDS:

Hotel heir Nicky Hilton
Actor Michael Wilding
Producer Mike Todd
Singer Eddie Fisher
Actor Richard Burton (married and divorced twice)
Senator John Warner
Teamster Larry Fortensky

SHORT-LIVED CELEB MARRIAGES

Britney Spears and Jason Allen	Less than 1 day
Dennis Hopper and Michelle Phillips	8 days
Drew Barrymore and Jeremy Thomas	1 month

Actors **Jude Law** and **Ewan McGregor** were once roommates.

CELEBRITY BABY NAMES

Courtney Cox and David Arquette	Coco
Gwyneth Paltrow and Chris Martin	Apple
Robert De Niro and Diahnne	Dreena
David and Victoria Beckham	Brooklyn
Madonna and Guy Ritchie	Rocco
Nicolas Cage and Alice Kim	Kal-El

Tom Cruise is dyslexic.

Johnny Depp was engaged to actresses Sherilyn Fenn, Jennifer Grey, and Winona Ryder, but never married any of the women.

Actor **Michael Douglas** flunked out of college.

Mia Farrow was on the cover of the first issue of *People* magazine, dated March 4, 1974.

Sally Field, Renee Zellweger, and **Kathie Lee Gifford** were all cheerleaders in high school.

81

NUMBERS

■ The **most common birthday** in the United States is October 5th.

■ A **duodecillion** has 39 zeros.

▌To convert degrees **Fahrenheit** to degrees **Celsius**, subtract 32 degrees and divide by 1.8.

▌To convert degrees **Celsius** to degrees **Fahrenheit**, multiply degrees by 1.8 and add 32 degrees.

▌The **Euro** is the currency for:

Belgium
Germany
Greece
Spain
France
Ireland
Italy
Luxembourg
The Netherlands
Austria
Portugal
Finland

ROMAN NUMERALS

1	I
2	II
3	III
4	IV
5	V
10	X
50	L
500	D
100	C
1,000	M

83

In 2100 B.C. a system based on the number 60, called a **sexagesimal system,** was developed in Babylonia. Today we measure seconds, minutes, and hours based on such a system.

The **first federal census** in the U.S. was in 1790. A population of 3,929,625 (which included 697,624 slaves) was recorded for 17 states.

Of the **total population in Hawaii**, 75% live on the island of O'ahu.

GEOMETRIC FIGURE	NUMBER OF SIDES
Triangle	3
Quadrilateral (square, rectangle, trapezoid, rhombus)	4
Pentagon	5
Hexagon	6
Octagon	8
Decagon	10
Dodecagon	12

The **population of Martha's Vineyard** increases from approximately 15,000 in the winter to over 100,000 in the summer.

The **first census in London** was taken in 1801. The population was documented at 959,000.

Mensa was founded by Roland Berrill and Dr. Lance Ware in England in 1946. To become a member of Mensa, you must score in the top 2% of the population on an approved test. Members of Mensa are called Mensans. There are over 100,000 Mensans in the world.

A **baker's dozen** equals a count of 13.

The **first written counting system** is credited to the Sumerians of Mesopotamia over 5,000 years ago.

A day is **23.934 hours** long.

WORD	TIME PERIOD
Semicentennial	50 years
Centennial	100 years
Sesquicentennial	150 years
Bicentennial	200 years
Quadricentennial	400 years
Quincentennial	500 years

A **gross** equals twelve dozen.

Monaco is the country with the biggest percentage of elderly people. Over 20% of the country's population is over the age of 65.

Rhode Island is the smallest state (by area) in the United States. It comprises only 1,231 square miles.

The country of **Andorra** has the highest life expectancy rate: the average is 83.5 years.

Marathon races are 26.2 miles long.

The **Dewey decimal system**, used to classify books and publications, uses the numbers 000 to 999. It is named after its inventor, Melvil Dewey.

The **minimum wage** was instituted in the United States in 1938; the rate originally was 25 cents an hour.

The average **human head** has approximately 100,000 hairs.

1 inch = 0.0245 meter

The first-known use of the **numeral zero** occurred in India in A.D. 876.

The **freezing point** of water is 32° Fahrenheit (0° Celsius).

85

■ The **boiling point of water** is 212° Fahrenheit (100° C).

■ **Pi**, the ratio of the circumference of a circle to its diameter, requires an infinite number of digits to give its exact value. Its value to eight decimal places is 3.14159265.

■ **IQs** (intelligence quotients) between 90 and 120 are considered average.

■ An **acute angle** measures more than 0 degrees but less than 90 degrees.

■ An **obtuse angle** measures more than 90 degrees but less than 180 degrees.

■ A **right angle** measures 90 degrees.

■ The average adult **human brain** weighs 3 pounds.

■ The average **human heart** beats 100,800 times per day.

■ The **lowest common denominator** is the smallest number that can be evenly divided into two other numbers.

■ The **Washington Monument** is 555 feet, 5-1/8 inches tall.

■ The **Mason-Dixon line** is located at 39° 43'26".

■ An **acre** is 43,560 square feet.

AMERICAN CURRENCY NOTE	FACE ON BILL
$1	George Washington
$2	Thomas Jefferson
$5	Abraham Lincoln
$10	Alexander Hamilton
$20	Andrew Jackson
$50	Ulysses Grant
$100	Benjamin Franklin
$500	William McKinley
$1000	Grover Cleveland
$5000	James Madison
$10,000	Salmon P. Chase
$100,000	Woodrow Wilson

More than half a million gallons of water go over **Niagara Falls** every second.

The **Peloponnesian War**, in which Sparta defeated Athens, lasted from 431 to 404 B.C.

The **Hoover Dam** in Nevada is 760-feet high.

At 55 stories, the **Woolworth Building** in New York City was the tallest building in the world from 1913 to 1930.

The **average life expectancy** in the U.S. in 1920 was 54 years.

There were 13 million **teenagers** in the United States in the mid-1950s.

▌ The famed **MIT** (Massachusetts Institute of Technology) admitted its first students in 1865.

▌ The first patent for a **fax machine** was given to Scottish inventor Alexander Bain in 1843.

▌ The **cash register** was invented in 1879.

▌ **Thermometers** were invented in the sixteenth century.

▌ **eBay**® was started in 1995 as auctionweb.com by Pierre Omidyar.

▌ The first **oil well** in the United States was drilled in Titusville, Pennsylvania in 1859.

▌ The Windows version of **AOL**® was launched in January 1993.

▌ The **silicon chip** was introduced in the United States in 1965.

▌ **Google**™ was founded by Larry Page and Sergey Brin. They met when they were both graduate students in Computer Science at Stanford University.

▌ Networking site **friendster**® was founded in California's Bay Area in 2002 by Jonathan Abrams and boasts over 20 million members.

▌ The popular web service **Earthlink**® was founded by Sky Dayton in March of 1994.

▌ According to the *Guinness Book of World Records*, the **most expensive cell phone** is a $104,050 phone designed by David Morris International of London. The phone is made of 18-carat gold, adorned with pink and gold diamonds.

The popular **craigslist** was founded by Craig Newmark in San Francisco in 1995 as a way to tell people in the city about events. Today, the site receives over 3 billion page views each month and posts listings from cities all over the world including Lima, Stockholm, and Boise.

The country with the **most Internet users** is the United States, followed by Japan.

The first **Atari**® game was Pong (1972).

Peter Merholz is credited with coming up with the term **"blog."**

Norman Joseph Woodland and Bernard Silver patented the **Universal Product Code** (UPC) in October 1952. It was later improved and adapted by David J. Collins in the late 1950s to track railroad cars. It wasn't until the early 1970s that UPCs were regularly scanned in grocery stores.

URL stands for Uniform Resource Locator.

Bandwidth is the amount of information that can be transmitted through cyberspace in an amount of time.

A **megahertz** equals 1 million electrical cycles per second.

HISTORY

In 1892—the 400th anniversary of **Columbus's arrival in the New World**—there were 63 million people in the United States. Seventeen million of them lived west of the Mississippi. Ninety years earlier, when Thomas Jefferson purchased the Louisiana Territory, he had estimated it would take a "hundred generations" for the United States to people the West—it had taken less than five.

The first **Soviet nuclear test** took place in 1949.

The **Salem Witch Trials** occurred in Massachusetts in 1692; 140 people were accused of witchcraft, of whom 20 were executed and 4 died in jail.

Jamestown, the first permanent New World British colony, was founded in 1607 in Virginia.

Rhode Island was founded by Roger Williams in 1636. Williams had been driven out of Boston for religious and political reasons.

Rhode Island became the **first British colony to outlaw slavery** in 1652.

The tenth President of the United States, **John Tyler**, assumed office in 1841 after William Henry Harrison died from pneumonia. He was the first Vice President to take office after a sitting president died.

Virginia Dare was the first child born of English parents in the New World on **August 18, 1587**. Her mother was Eleanor White and her father was Anania Dare. Her grandfather was Governor John White of Roanoke, Virginia.

Richmond, Virginia was the capital of the Confederacy.

Margaret Leech was the first woman to receive the Pulitzer Prize for history. The prize was awarded for her book *Reveille in Washington* in 1942. In 1960, she became the only woman to receive the Pulitzer Prize for history twice. She won with her book *In the Days of McKinley*.

The **Boston Tea Party** took place in 1773. In 1774, the Intolerable Acts (as the colonists called them) were passed, barring the use of Boston Harbor until the tea was paid for.

Charlemagne was the first emperor of the Holy Roman Empire.

The **Titanic** sank in the early hours of April 15, 1912.

The **Trojan War** is thought to have started around 1200 B.C.

The city of **Pompeii** in Italy was destroyed in A.D. 79 when Vesuvius erupted, killing more than 10,000 people.

The **United States** dropped the first atomic bomb on Hiroshima, Japan on August 6, 1945.

Montezuma was emperor of the Aztecs from 1502 to 1520.

The **Crusades** were wars fought between the late eleventh and thirteenth centuries.

Julius Caesar was assassinated on March 15, 44 B.C.

Cleopatra was the queen of Egypt from 51 to 30 B.C.

Attila the Hun was the king of the Huns from A.D. 434 to 453.

The **original Thirteen States** were:

Delaware
Pennsylvania
New Jersey
Georgia
Connecticut
Massachusetts
Maryland
South Carolina
New Hampshire
Virginia
New York
North Carolina
Rhode Island

The **Liberty Bell** (cast in Philadelphia) is said to have cracked on July 8, 1835 when it was tolling the death of Chief Justice John Marshall.

The stars and stripes pattern of the **American flag** was designed by Francis Hopkinson.

Englishwoman **Florence Nightingale** was nicknamed "Lady with the Lamp," because of her day-and-night care of British soldiers in the Crimean War.

"Manifest Destiny" was a slogan in the 1840s in the United States meaning that the country was destined to expand to the Pacific Ocean.

It was Thomas Paine who originated the phrase "These are times that try men's souls." The text appeared in the first of a series of pamphlets entitled **The American Crisis**, which Paine started publishing in 1776.

Prohibition lasted in the United States from 1920 to 1933. Alcoholic beverages were made illegal throughout the country by the eighteenth amendment to the Constitution, which was repealed in 1933.

The first postage stamp was issued in Great Britain in 1840. It was known as the **Penny Black**.

The Great Depression began in America on October 29, 1929, a day now referred to as **Black Tuesday**.

Ellis Island, in New York City harbor, was the main immigration station for the United States from 1892 to 1943.

Pu Yi was two years old when he became the Emperor of China in 1908. He was six when he abdicated his throne.

The empress **Catherine the Great's** (1729-1796) name was Sophie Auguste Fredericke von Anhalt-Zerbst.

The **great fire of London** was in 1666.

Valley Forge, the quarters for the American Army for part of the Revolutionary War (1777-1778), is a valley in Eastern Pennsylvania.

The first **United States paper money** was printed in 1862.

The first satellite to orbit Earth was the Soviet spacecraft **Sputnik I**, in 1957.

The states of **North Dakota, South Dakota, Montana,** and **Washington** all were admitted into the Union on the same day: February 22, 1889.

Expeditioners **Lewis and Clark** were sent by President Thomas Jefferson to explore the western lands of the United States. They set out from St. Louis, Missouri on May 14, 1804 and finished on September 23, 1806. The trail covered 3,700 miles and followed the Missouri and Columbia Rivers. Today the trail runs through Indiana, Illinois, Missouri, Kansas, Nebraska, South Dakota, North Dakota, Montana, Idaho, Oregon, and Washington.

The first American woman to cast a ballot to vote was **Louisa Swain** on Sept. 6, 1870.

The **Thirty Years War**, which redrew the map of Germany and involved much of the European continent, was fought from 1618 to 1648.

The **first foreign aid bill** was passed by Congress in 1812. The funds were for earthquake relief in Venezuela.

Susan B. Anthony and Elizabeth Cady Stanton founded the **National Woman Suffrage Association** on May 15, 1869. They campaigned for the voting rights of women.

In 1780, **Pennsylvania** became the first state in America to abolish slavery.

The **Department of Agriculture** was created by Congress in 1862.

Hawaii became the 50th state of the United States on August 21, 1959.

South Carolina became the first state to secede from the Union on December 20, 1860.

The **Louisiana Purchase** was made on April 30, 1803. The land the U.S. bought from France for 15 million dollars stretched from the Mississippi River to the Rocky Mountains and from the Gulf of Mexico to the Canadian border. It doubled the size of the U.S. at that time.

In 1973 the U.S. ended the **military draft** that had been in place since before the country's entry into World War II.

The **Pony Express** ran from April 3, 1860 through October 1861.

Gold was found as a chance discovery by James Marshall at Sutter's Mill in California on January 24, 1848, beginning what would become known as the **California Gold Rush**.

Sheriff Pat Garrett shot and killed **William H. Bonney** (a.k.a. Billy the Kid) on July 14, 1881, ending the Kid's six-year reign as one of the deadliest and most notorious outlaws of the Wild West.

Between 1890 and 1904, the population of **Los Angeles** quadrupled to nearly 200,000. But it was William Mulholland and Fred Eaton who helped boost the population boom with irrigation systems that brought water from Owens Valley to the Los Angeles basin by 1913, turning Los Angeles into the most powerful city on the West Coast.

Those walking along Broadway (at West 204th Street) in Manhattan may be surprised to come across an intact farmhouse. The **Dyckman House** is the only surviving 18th-century farmhouse in the borough. The structure was built in 1783.

Los Angeles saw its **first Buddhist temple** built in July of 1904.

There were 76 million babies born between 1946 and 1964. The people born during this time are known as the **baby boomers**.

Annie Oakley married Frank E. Butler when she was 15 years old.

The Hundred Years' War between England and France lasted from 1337 to 1453.

Civil War general **Robert E. Lee** attended West Point Academy with many of the Union Army generals he fought against in the Civil War. He had been asked to head the northern army but declined because his home state, Virginia, was part of the Confederacy.

SPORTS

The five interlocked rings of the **Olympics** represent:

Africa
North & South America
Asia
Australia
Europe

THE FIRST FIVE MODERN SUMMER OLYMPICS WERE HELD:

1896	Athens, Greece
1900	Paris, France
1904	St. Louis, Missouri (USA)
1908	London, England
1912	Stockholm, Sweden

THE FIRST FIVE MODERN WINTER OLYMPICS WERE HELD:

1924	Chamonix, France
1928	St. Moritz, Switzerland
1932	Lake Placid, New York (USA)
1936	Garmisch-Partenkirchen, Germany
1948	St. Moritz, Switzerland

The **New York Cosmos** were the first American soccer team that Pelé played for.

The four major **tennis championships** are:

The French Open
Wimbledon
The Australian Open
The U.S. Open

Contrary to popular belief, **Abner Doubleday** did not invent baseball. The game was developed from street ball-and-stick games played in the United States.

To fish with a rod is called **angling**.

97

Famous horse **Seabiscuit** beat horse War Admiral in a match race. The legendary race took place on November 1, 1938 at Pimlico Race Course in Baltimore, Maryland.

The names of the **Triple Crown Races** are:

The Kentucky Derby
The Preakness Stakes
The Belmont Stakes

ATHLETE NICKNAMES

Reggie Jackson (baseball)	Mr. October
Julius Erving (basketball)	Dr. J.
Wilt Chamberlain (basketball)	Wilt the Stilt
William Perry (football)	The Fridge
Joe Jackson (baseball)	Shoeless Joe
Karl Malone (basketball)	The Mailman
Lou Gehrig (baseball)	The Iron Horse

Wayne Gretzky scored the most goals by an individual in a hockey season. He scored 92 goals in the 1981/82 season for the Edmonton Oilers.

Three goals scored by one player in hockey or soccer is called a **"hat trick."**

A **royal flush** (Ace, King, Queen, Jack, and 10 of the same suit) is the best possible hand in poker.

The **first U.S. intercollegiate athletic competition** took place in August 1852. Harvard competed against Yale in a rowing race.

A **bowler** needs 12 consecutive strikes to score a perfect game.

1912 was the last year **Olympic gold medals** were made entirely out of gold.

A hockey player spends 10 minutes in the **penalty box** for a misconduct penalty.

The first **bike race** to go from town to town ran from Paris to Rouen in 1868.

The first person to climb the 14,692-foot **Matterhorn** mountain peak in Switzerland was Edward Whymper. The year was 1865.

Basketball was invented in 1891 by Dr. James Naismith in Springfield, Massachusetts.

The first rules of **badminton** were established in England in 1895.

Extreme sports you may not have heard of:

Buildering (climbing the outside of buildings)
Wakeboarding (a combination of surfing, snowboarding, and waterskiing)
Bouldering (climbing boulders without a rope)

Babe Ruth's given name was George Herman Ruth.

Hauling moonshine in the hills of North Carolina and racing were one and the same for **Junior Johnson**, celebrated as "the Last American Hero" by novelist Tom Wolfe. He was never caught driving but was eventually busted in 1956 working at the family still. Johnson spent nearly a year in jail for making illegal whiskey but became the first and only ex-felon to win the Daytona 500 in 1960.

The **Indianapolis 500** is the best-attended single-day sporting event in the world. Over 500,000 spectators attend it each year.

Indianapolis Motor Speedway is the largest sports venue in the world. It hosted its first motor racing event in 1909 and the first Indy 500 race in 1911.

The first **Super Bowl** (the championship game of the National Football League) was played in 1967.

On August 6, 1926, **Gertrude Ederle** became the first woman to swim the English Channel.

The **Boston Red Sox**, then called the Pilgrims, won the first World Series which took place in October, 1903. They defeated the Pittsburgh Pirates.

There are four **major golf tournaments**:

The Masters
The U.S. Open
The British Open
The PGA

There are more **tennis courts** per capita in Vermont than anywhere else in the U.S.

Soccer is played with eleven players on each team.

The game we know as **Scrabble**® was invented by Alfred Mosher Butts, an architect, in 1938. It was based on Lexico, another game invented by Butts.

Jackie Robinson became the first black person to play baseball in the major leagues in America on April 15, 1947.

In **professional basketball**, quarters are twelve minutes long.

The first **World Cup** (soccer) was held in 1930 in Uruguay. The United States team was one of only thirteen countries that participated.

A goal in **rugby** is worth six points.

The **first professional basketball game** was played in 1896 in Trenton, New Jersey.

In **field hockey**, a player must hit the ball with the flat side of his/her stick.

The first **Olympic Games** to include women were held in Paris in 1900.

World Championships for **judo** were first held in 1956.

NUMBER OF BOXING ROUNDS:

Amateur	3
Professional	12
Title fights	15

When a **diver** does a handstand on the platform before diving off, it's called an armstand dive.

A player is not allowed to use more than fourteen clubs per game in **golf**.

Baseball has nine fielding positions:

First baseman
Second baseman
Third baseman
Shortstop
Left Fielder
Center Fielder
Right Fielder
Pitcher
Catcher

In 1992, athlete **Deion Sanders** played in a World Series baseball game and an NFL football game in the same week.

RACING

In 2005, 24-year-old Formula 1 racecar driver **Fernando Alonso** of Spain became the youngest racer to win the world driving championship.

Record six-time Formula 1 champion **Michael Schumacher** is the highest paid race-car driver in the world, earning $80 million annually.

Street Tires vs. **Race Tires**
Street Tire
Width: about 8"
Weight: 33 lbs
Lifetime: about 80,000 miles

Indy Race Tire
Width: 14"
Weight: 22 lbs
Lifetime: 100 miles

A **Top Fuel dragster** accelerates from 0 to 100 mph in less than 0.8-seconds; this produces a force nearly five times that of gravity.

The **Indianapolis 500** is run on Memorial Day every year.

NASCAR stands for The National Association for Stock Car Auto Racing. It was founded in Daytona Beach, Florida in 1947.

Richard Petty has more stock car racing victories—200—than any other driver in NASCAR Cup history.

The worst crash in auto racing history occurred at the Le Mans road course in northwest France in 1955 when a Mercedes Benz race car being driven by **Pierre Levegh** hit a bank (avoiding a slower car) by the grandstand and immediately exploded. Parts of the wreckage were blown into the enclosure, claiming 77 lives and injuring 77 other people.

Stock car driver **Alan Kulwicki's** first NASCAR win came at Phoenix International Raceway in 1988, and it was there that he made his first clockwise post-race celebration lap. He went on to win the 1992 Championship, but was tragically killed in a small plane crash in spring 1993.

Four-time Indianapolis 500 winner **A.J. Foyt** won a record 67 Indy Car races during his career, and captured seven Indy Car championships, also a record.

During his career, racecar driver **Richie Evans** won a record nine NASCAR national Modified titles, including an unbeatable eight in a row (1978-1985).

The **first long-distance car race** was in 1901. The race was a 464-mile course from New York City to Buffalo. The winner drove an average speed of 15 m.p.h.

FASHION

The über-expensive and highly sought after **Birkin bag** was named after actress and singer Jane Birkin.

Fashion designer **Donna Karan** was fired from her first job with designer Anne Klein.

Mary Kay® Cosmetics has over 1.3 million beauty consultants.

Mary Phelps Jacob patented the **first modern brassiere** in 1914.

Ralph Lauren, who never attended fashion school, started his popular Polo label in 1967.

Musician **Sade** studied fashion design in London. Her designs were featured in British band Spandau Ballet's first appearance in the United States.

Orlando Pita of the salon Orlo in Manhattan garnered attention for his high price tag: $800 for a haircut.

The **Kelly bag** was named after Oscar-winning actress Grace Kelly.

The **Language of Fashion** is the first dictionary compiled by a woman. Mary Brooks Picken assembled its 8,000 entries in 1939.

The **mullet** has been worn by famous folks including Michael Bolton, Brad Pitt, and David Bowie.

1960's mega-model **Twiggy** was born Leslie Hornby. She was given the nickname Twiggy, because of her thin frame.

Coco Chanel named her perfume **Chanel No. 5** because five was her lucky number.

There is no known documentation of when **people first wore hats**.

SEX

The **Kinsey Institute** was founded in Indiana in 1947. The 2004 film *Kinsey*, starring Liam Neeson, was based on the life of institute founder Dr. Alfred C. Kinsey.

The average length of an **erect male penis** is 6".

The popular HBO series **Sex in the City** began its first season with the female characters deciding to start "having sex like men."

Condoms have been traced back to ancient Egypt, when linen sheaths were used for contraception.

There are approximately 200-300 million **sperm cells** in the average male ejaculation.

The **Kama Sutra** is said to possibly have been written in the first-century A.D. It was translated into English and published by Sir Richard Francis Burton in 1883.

Sexual Behavior in the Human Male—the famous Kinsey Report—was published on January 5, 1948. *Sexual Behavior in the Human Female* was not published until 1953.

At **fertilization** of a human egg, the female supplies an X-chromosome. The male can contribute an X- or Y-chromosome. If the male sperm provides an X-chromosome, the baby will be a female.

Planned Parenthood, established in 1942, was formed from the National Birth Control League, founded in 1916 by Margaret Sanger.

Overall birth rates have been declining in the United States since 1965.

- In **Arizona** it is illegal to have more than two dildos in a house.

- It is also illegal in Arizona for a **secretary** to be alone with his/her boss.

- In **Oklahoma** you must be married in order to have sex legally.

- It is illegal to kiss for more than 5 minutes in **Iowa**.

- In **Indiana** it is illegal to be in a state of sexual arousal in public.

- Talking "dirty" during sex is illegal in **Oregon**.

- **Pornography** is Greek for "the writings of prostitutes."

- Sexual intercourse between **chimpanzees** lasts, on average, 3 seconds.

BUSINESS

■ The first **Holiday Inn®** was opened in Memphis, Tennessee in 1952.

▌**Vogue** magazine began as a New York weekly society publication in 1892. The cover price was 10 cents.

■ The **National Minimum Wage Act** was enacted on June 25, 1938.

▌Famed magazine editor **Tina Brown** was kicked out of three boarding schools by the time she was 16 years old.

▌The average American works **nine weeks** more per year than the average European.

■ Doris and Don Fisher opened the first **Gap®** store in San Francisco in 1969.

■ Ninety-nine percent of **dental hygienists** are women.

▌Mega-store chain **Target's®** weekly advertising circular was the second most read insert in U.S. newspapers in 1985. The most read insert was the Sunday comics.

▌Fast-food chain **Burger King®** started as one restaurant, Insta-Burger King, in Miami, Florida in 1957. Today there are over 11,000 restaurants worldwide.

■ **Samuel Cole** opened the first tavern in Boston on March 4, 1634.

▌The **Fair Labor Standards Act** of 1938, which established the 40-hour work week, went into effect in 1941.

The first organized **labor strike** recorded in the U.S. was in 1786. The printers of Philadelphia called a strike for higher wages.

Media guru **Martha Stewart** was a model and stockbroker before making a living as a domestic diva.

There is a **McDonald's**® museum in Des Plaines, Illinois. It is a re-creation of the first McDonald's, which opened in the city on April 15, 1955.

Bandleader Fred Waring developed the **Waring Blender** to mix daiquiris.

The **Apple Computer Company** was founded by Stephen Wozniak and Steven Jobs in 1976.

The **NASDAQ** stands for The National Association of Security Dealers Automated Quotations. It was founded in 1971.

The **New York Stock Exchange** is located on Wall Street in Manhattan.

EEC stands for the European Economic Community. It was established in 1957 to promote free trade. The founding members were:

Belgium
France
Italy
Luxembourg
The Netherlands
West Germany

The **European Union**, formally established in 1993, includes the following countries:

Austria
Belgium
Cyprus
Czech Republic
Denmark
Estonia
Finland
France
Germany
Greece
Hungary
Ireland

Italy
Latvia
Lithuania
Luxembourg
Malta
The Netherlands
Poland
Portugal
Slovakia
Slovenia
Spain
Sweden
United Kingdom

The leading industrial nations in the world are known as the
Great Eight (or G8). They are:

Great Britain
Canada
France
Germany
Italy
Japan
Russia
United States

INVENTIONS

■ **Self-winding clocks** were invented in 1783.

■ **Bottle caps** were invented in 1892.

■ **Contact lenses** were invented in 1924.

The Samuel Morse house, once home to the inventor of the **Morse code**, is in Poughkeepsie, New York.

Benjamin Franklin's famous kite-flying expedition in a thunderstorm, in which he proved lightning is electricity, took place in 1752.

The grandfather of beat writer William Seward Burroughs, also named William Seward Burroughs, founded the **Burroughs Adding Machine** company, which evolved into the Burroughs Corporation.

The inventor of **earmuffs**, Chester Greenwood, was 15 years old when he developed the idea in 1873. He was 18 years old when he obtained the patent.

■ **Eyeglasses** are generally no longer made of glass.

LEONARDO DA VINCI PRODUCED DESIGNS FOR THE FOLLOWING INVENTIONS:
Submarine
Tank
Cluster bomb
Glider
Calculator
Car

Albert Einstein's **"Special Theory of Relativity"** was published in 1905. His "General Theory of Relativity" was published in 1915.

Xerography, the process behind the photocopy machine, was invented by Chester Carlson in 1938.

George de Mestral invented **Velcro**® in 1948.

Nylon stockings were first sold in the United States in 1940.

Roller skates were invented by Joseph Merlin of Belgium in 1760.

The first woman to apply for a United States patent was **Mary Kies,** in May, 1809. Her patent was for a method of weaving straw with silk.

Inventor **Thomas Edison**, whose numerous inventions include the phonograph (1878) and the incandescent light bulb (1879), also invented talking dolls (1890).

Invention of the first **motorcycle** is usually attributed to American Sylvester Howard Roper. He built one with a steam-powered engine in 1867.

Badminton was named after the house (Badminton House) where the game was played by the Duke of Beaufort in 1870.

Otto Hahn and Fritz Strassman of Germany first demonstrated **nuclear fission** in 1939.

CinemaScope, the widescreen cinema technique, was introduced by Twentieth Century Fox in 1953. The first CinemaScope film was *The Robe*.

Touch-tone telephones were introduced in 1964.

Air conditioning was invented by Willis H. Carrier in 1902.

The **first lead pencils** had no erasers.

HEALTH

The **spine** consists of 24 vertebrae, not including the 5 fused vertebrae of the sacrum and the 4 fused vertebrae of the coccyx.

In the average person, the human **heart beats** 60-80 times per minute when the body is at rest.

Movement of each human **eye** is controlled by six extraocular muscles.

Weight Watchers® was founded in 1963 by Jean Nidetch who invited women to her home in Queens, N.Y. to talk about weight loss.

Morphine is made from opium.

FEARS

Hydrophobia	Water
Gephyrophobia	Crossing bridges
Triskaidekaphobia	Number 13
Mysophobia	Germs
Ophidiophobia	Snakes

One out of 585 births in the United States is a **triplet birth**.

The **first successful heart transplant** was performed on December 3, 1976 by Dr. Christian Barnard at Groote Shuur Hospital in Cape Town, South Africa. The patient was Louis Washkansky. He survived for eighteen days.

According to the Centers for Disease Control, **obesity** accounts for 26,000 deaths a year in the United States.

The average American gains one pound during the holiday season.

When humans are at **rest**, 15% of their blood is in their brains.

Humans start to get their **teeth** around the age of six months.

The average adult **sleeps** seven hours a night during the work week.

Anna Freud (daughter of Sigmund Freud) studied the emotional life of children and wrote about her findings in *Normality and Pathology in Childhood* (1965).

Most people **dream** for two hours in an eight-hour night of sleep.

Curly hair is more likely to be passed down the generations than straight hair.

Skin is the largest human organ.

The average **newborn baby's head** takes up 1/4 of its body length; an adult's head makes up 1/8 of its height.

10 percent of people are **left-handed**.

Your **heart** is slightly larger than your own fist.

Adult humans have **206 bones**.

The average person in the United States **eats over 50 tons of food** in his or her lifetime.

A **newborn baby** can sleep up to 23 hours a day.

Wisdom teeth usually emerge in a person between the ages of 17 and 25.

The **1855 Farmers Almanac** included a recipe for toothpaste. Ingredients for the mixture include sage and honey.

One out of 200 people may be **allergic to nuts**.

Brazil nuts have approximately 2,500 times more selenium than other nuts.

Every year in the United States, nearly **1 of every 5 deaths** is related to smoking. Cigarettes kill more Americans than alcohol, car accidents, suicide, AIDS, homicide, and illegal drugs combined.

You should never feed a child under one-year of age honey. The baby could develop a disease known as **infant botulism**.

You can check your measure of leanness with the **BMI** (Body Mass Index). To do so multiply your height in inches by your height in inches. Divide your weight in pounds by the result. Now, multiply the resulting number by 703. If the number you get is over 25, you are considered overweight.

Identical twins do not have identical fingerprints.

Humans lose more than half of their **body heat** through the head.

The **femur** (thigh bone) is the longest bone in the human body.

The big toe is called the **hallux**.

Color blindness affects one in twelve men.

The **trachea** is also known as the windpipe.

The **human tongue** can detect up to five hundred tastes.

A normal **temperature** for humans is 98.6° Fahrenheit.

The **Red Cross** was founded by Henri Dunant in 1864.

Blood types are either A, B, AB, or O.

The **Centers for Disease Control and Prevention** (CDC), a government agency that monitors infectious diseases, has its headquarters in Atlanta, Georgia.

Physicians take the **Hippocratic oath** when they pledge to practice medicine.

Humans lose **10 cups of fluid** a day.

Medicare and **Medicaid** were established in 1965.

The **small intestine** is longer than the large intestine.

Fertility rates in women aged 35-49 in the United States have doubled since 1978.

The **first successful blood transfusion** was performed by James Blundell in 1818.

Fingerprints can be detected in the fetus at three months.

Sneezes can travel almost 100 m.p.h.

The **first blood bank** was established in 1937 in Chicago.

Clogged **sebaceous glands** (located in the skin) can cause pimples.

RELIGION

The major religion in Europe is **Christianity**. Most European Christians are Roman Catholics.

Founded by **Lord Baltimore** in 1634, Maryland became a safe haven for Catholics who were being persecuted in other colonies.

Bibles were first placed in hotel rooms in 1908 in the Superior Hotel in Iron Mountain, Montana.

PATRON SAINTS OF OCCUPATIONS

Housewives	St. Anne, Mother of the Virgin Mary
Paratroopers	St. Michael the Archangel
Pawnbrokers	St. Nicholas of Myra
Tax Collectors	St. Matthew the Apostle
Taxi Drivers	St. Fiacre

THE SEVEN DEADLY SINS:	THE SEVEN CARDINAL VIRTUES:
Pride	Prudence
Envy	Courage
Anger	Temperance
Sloth	Justice
Greed	Faith
Gluttony	Hope
Lust	Charity

John is the most popular name for popes.

Ash Wednesday is the seventh Wednesday before Easter.

Lent begins on Ash Wednesday and ends on Easter.

■ The Sunday before Easter is **Palm Sunday**.

■ Mormon **Joseph Smith** and **Brigham Young** were both born in Vermont.

■ The highest form of consciousness in Buddhism is known as **nirvana**.

▌Joseph Smith founded the **Mormon Church**—known officially as the Church of Jesus Christ of Latter-Day Saints—in 1830.

■ The **first synagogue** in North America was built in New York City in 1730.

■ The **first Catholic cathedral** in the United States was built in Baltimore in 1821.

▌The **Twelve Disciples** of Jesus were:

Andrew
Bartholomew
James the Greater
James the Lesser
John
Judas Iscariot
Judas, Son of James
Matthew
Simon Peter
Philip
Simon the Zealot
Thomas

▌London's **Westminster Abbey** houses the tomb of Henry III, who is credited with starting the reconstruction of the building in its current Gothic form in 1245.

▌The first Catholic mass given in English was performed in St. Louis, Missouri by **Reverend Frederick R. McManus** on August 24, 1964.

LITERATURE

Allen Ginsburg first read the famed poem **"Howl"** in public on October 1955 at the Six Gallery in San Francisco.

In 1841, **Edgar Allan Poe** made $800 a year working as an editor.

Famed mystery writer **Agatha Christie** (1892-1976) never attended school.

The first Nobel Prize for Literature was awarded to **Rene F. A. Sully Prudhomme** of France in 1901.

The appointed **poet laureate** of the United States receives an annual stipend of $35,000.

The often-quoted "Two roads diverged in a wood and I—I took the one less traveled by" is from Robert Frost's 1915 poem **"The Road Not Taken."**

J.D. Salinger is the author of the **Catcher in the Rye**. It was first published in book form in 1951.

Shakespeare's **Tragedies:**

Antony and Cleopatra
Coriolanus
Hamlet
Julius Caesar
King Lear
Macbeth
Othello
Romeo and Juliet
Timon of Athens
Titus Andronicus

Shakespeare's **Comedies** (including his Romances and Problem Plays):

All's Well That Ends Well
As You Like It
The Comedy of Errors
Cymbeline
Love's Labours Lost
Measure for Measure
The Merry Wives of Windsor
The Merchant of Venice
A Midsummer Night's Dream
Much Ado About Nothing
Pericles, Prince of Tyre
Taming of the Shrew
The Tempest
Troilus and Cressida
Twelfth Night
Two Gentlemen of Verona
Winter's Tale

National Novel Writing Month is November. The goal for participants, who start penning on November 1, is to write a 50,000 word novel by the stroke of midnight on November 30. The program was founded by NaNoWriMo in Oakland, California in 1999. There are over 250 chapters throughout the world.

Former **poet laureates** of the United States include Elizabeth Bishop, Robert Lowell, and Conrad Aiken. Iowa-born poet Ted Kooser was appointed the position in April 2005.

Jack London was the first writer to earn one million dollars from his writing.

F. Scott Fitzgerald's wife Zelda died in the Highland Hospital sanitarium in a fire in 1948.

Though she often wrote about courtship and marriage, author **Jane Austen** never married.

Though she often wrote about children, **Louisa May Alcott** never married or had children of her own.

Mary Shelley was only 19 years old when she wrote the story that would be published as **Frankenstein**.

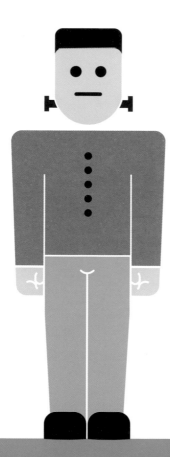

The three **Brontë sisters** wrote under the following pseudonyms:

Currer Bell (Charlotte)
Ellis Bell (Emily)
Acton Bell (Anne)

The 1939 novel **Gadsby** by Ernest Vincent Wright does not contain the letter "e."

The oft-quoted poem **"Kubla Khan,"** by Samuel Taylor Coleridge, was supposedly never finished because someone knocked on the poet's door during its composition and he lost his inspiration.

Scientific American is the oldest continuously published magazine in the United States. It was first published in 1845.

To the Lighthouse, by English author Virginia Woolf, was first published in 1927.

The lines **"Water, water every where,/Nor any drop to drink"** are from "The Rime of the Ancient Mariner" by Samuel Taylor Coleridge.

Theodor Seuss Geisel is more commonly known as **Dr. Seuss**.

Little Men, the sequel to Louisa May Alcott's novel *Little Women* (1868-1869), was published in 1871.

The phrase "Parting is such sweet sorrow" is from Shakespeare's play **Romeo and Juliet**.

The **Old Globe Theater** in London is where many of William Shakespeare's plays were first performed.

The ancient Roman poet Ovid wrote the **Metamorphoses**. The Czech author Franz Kafka wrote **The Metamorphosis**.

Sinclair Lewis was the first American to win the Nobel Prize for literature in December 1930.

The novel **The Brothers Karamazov** by Fyodor Dostoevsky was first published in serial form in Russia between 1879 and 1880. It was not translated into English until 1912.

Ebenezer Scrooge is the miser in Charles Dickens's story **A Christmas Carol** (1843).

Willie Loman is the salesman in Arthur Miller's Pulitzer Prize-winning play **Death of a Salesman** (1949).

The novel **Anna Karenina** (1873-1876) was written by Leo Tolstoy.

The fairy tale **"Sleeping Beauty"** was written by Charles Perrault.

Sherwood Forest, the home of Robin Hood, is an actual forest in England.

There are 24 tales in Chaucer's **Canterbury Tales**.

The classic tale **"The Princess and the Pea"** was written by Hans Christian Andersen in 1835.

The mythological **Pandora's box** was given to Pandora by Zeus.

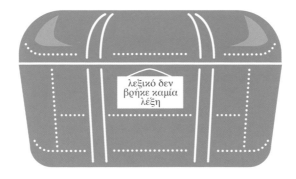

THE GREEKS AND ROMANS USUALLY GAVE DIFFERENT NAMES TO THE SAME GODS AND GODDESSES. HERE ARE A DOZEN:

GREEK	ROMAN	ATTRIBUTE
Aphrodite	Venus	goddess of love
Apollo	Apollo	god of the sun
Artemis	Diana	goddess of the moon
Ares	Mars	god of war
Athena	Minerva	goddess of wisdom
Dionysus	Bacchus	god of wine
Eros	Cupid	god of love
Hermes	Mercury	messenger of the gods
Hades	Pluto	god of the underworld
Poseidon	Neptune	god of the sea
Persephone	Proserpina	goddess of the underworld
Zeus	Jupiter	king of the gods

Betty Friedan is the author of **The Feminine Mystique** (1963), a book integral to the women's movement of the 1960s.

Writers who expose corruption in government and other organizations are known as **muckrakers**.

Dale Carnegie is the author of the 1936 book *How to Win Friends and Influence People*.

Shakespeare's longest play is **Hamlet**. It has 3,901 lines of text.

In Europe, all types of popular literature were once called **"romance."**

Moby-Dick, written by Herman Melville, was published in 1851.

Shakespeare's sonnets consist of 154 poems.

Poet **Carl Sandburg** held various odd jobs including shining shoes, washing dishes, delivering milk, and working as a fireman.

127

Poet and writer **Maya Angelou** was the first female black fare collector with the San Francisco Streetcar Company.

The real name of **Lewis Carroll**, author of *Alice in Wonderland*, is Charles Lutwidge Dodson.

Mark Twain and Charles Dudley Warner collaborated on the 1873 novel **The Gilded Age**. The name of the era refers to the large fortunes people amassed through corruption.

Poet **Williams Carlos Williams** received a medical degree from the University of Pennsylvania in 1906 and worked as a physician and writer.

George Eliot, author of *Middlemarch*, was a woman.

Writer **James Baldwin** was once a minister.

Famous beat writer **Jack Kerouac** (*On the Road*) was once an altar boy (1932).

Helen of Troy was considered the most beautiful woman in the world in Greek mythology.

Geoffrey Chaucer, author of *The Canterbury Tales*, introduced iambic pentameter into English poetry.

The **Victorian Era** in literature is considered to have spanned the years 1832 to 1901.

Jack Kerouac is buried in the Edsom Cemetery in Lowell, Massachusetts. He died in 1969.

Playwright **Edward Albee** was adopted.

The **World Almanac** made its debut in 1868.

The famed **Chelsea Hotel** was built in 1884. Writers Dylan Thomas, Arthur Miller, and Vladimir Nabokov all lived there.

Independent bookstore **City Lights** (San Francisco, CA) was founded by Lawrence Ferlinghetti and Peter D. Martin in 1953. City Lights was the first to publish Ginsburg's "Howl."

Writer **George Plimpton** founded (along with H. L. Humes and Peter Matthiessen) the prestigious literary journal, *The Paris Review,* in 1953.

The prestigious artists community **Yaddo** is located in Saratoga Springs, New York.

Novelist **Herman Melville** (*Moby-Dick*) took up whaling at the age of 21 on the whaler *Acushnet*.

Edna St. Vincent Millay lived in the narrowest house in New York City. Today, there is a plaque on the house on Grove Street in the West Village of Manhattan. The house is approximately 9-feet wide.

Reuter's news service began by delivering information with carrier pigeons.

O. Henry is the pen name for William Sydney Porter.

Writer **William Saroyan** was born in Fresno, California. His granddaughter, Strawberry Saroyan, wrote a memoir entitled *Girl Walks into a Bar* (2003).

Novelists **Truman Capote** (*Breakfast at Tiffany's*) and **Harper Lee** (*To Kill a Mockingbird*) were life-long friends.

MUSIC

Jazz singer Billie Holiday's autobiography **Lady Sings the Blues** was published in 1956.

Pop singer **Ashlee Simpson** (sister of pop singer and *Newlyweds* star Jessica Simpson) was the youngest person admitted into the School of American Ballet.

The origin of New York City's nickname **"The Big Apple"** is not certain, but it was popularized by jazz musicians who felt that you hadn't achieved fame until you played New York City. They believed there were many apples on the tree of success, but NYC was the big one.

The bandleader on the "Late Show with David Letterman" is **Paul Shaffer**.

Elvis Presley was born on January 8, 1935. His twin brother, Jesse Garon Presley, was stillborn.

John Lennon and **Yoko Ono** were married in Gibraltar in 1969. They spent their honeymoon in a "bed-in" to promote world peace in their hotel room Amsterdam. The press was invited for 12-hour periods to the hotel room each day.

The main female singer in an opera is known as a **prima donna**.

Jimi Hendrix's middle name was Marshall. He also used Marshall amps. And his chief photographer was ace shooter Jim Marshall. He died at the age of 27 in 1970.

The **phonograph** was invented by Thomas Edison in 1877.

Each year, 650 million people watch the **Grammy awards**.

Dorothy Fields was the first woman to win an Academy Award for songwriting. The year was 1937. She shared the Oscar with composer Jerome Kern for her lyrics to the song "The Way You Look Tonight," which was in the Fred Astaire and Ginger Rogers film *Swing Time*. Later, Fields became the first woman to be elected to the Songwriter's Hall of Fame. The year was 1971.

Musician **David Bowie** was born David Jones.

George M. Cohan wrote the song **"Yankee Doodle Dandy."**

Singer-songwriter **Jackson Browne** was raised in Los Angeles, but was born in Heidelberg, Germany.

A **string quartet** includes two violins, a viola, and a cello.

An **operetta** is a light-hearted opera.

An **octave** is an interval between tones.

The **viola** has a lower-pitched sound than the violin.

Folksinger **Woody Guthrie** wrote the song "This Land is Your Land," in 1940, in response to Irving Berlin's song "God Bless America."

Giacomo Puccini compossed the opera *Madame Butterfly*.

Ludwig van Beethoven continued to compose music even after going deaf.

The song **"Camptown Races"** was written by Stephen Foster.

The original members of the band **Buffalo Springfield** (formed in 1966) included Neil Young, Stephen Stills, Richie Furay, Bruce Palmer, Dewey Martin, and Jim Messina.

Jimi Hendrix was born and buried in **Seattle, Washington**.

The Four Tops were Levi Stubbs, Abdul "Duke" Fakir, Renaldo "Obie" Benson, and Lawrence Payton, Jr.

THE REAL NAMES OF THE FOUR ORIGINAL RAMONES:

Joey	Jeffrey Hyman
Johnny	John Cummings
Dee Dee	Douglas Glen Colvin
Tommy	Thomas Erdelyi

The **"Grand Ole Opry"** variety show debuted in 1925.

The Pointer Sisters, **McGuire Sisters**, and **Fontaine Sisters** are all groups really comprised of sisters. No members of the group **Twisted Sister** are actual sisters—or women.

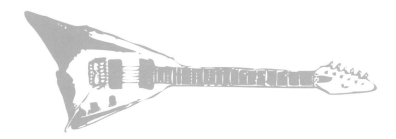

The phrase **"rock and roll"** was coined by Cleveland disc jockey Alan Freed in 1951.

German composer **Carl Philipp Emanuel Bach** was the music director of five churches.

Bands **Eric Clapton** has played in:

The Roosters
Casey Jones and the Engineers
The Yardbirds
John Mayall's Bluesbreakers
Cream
Blind Faith
Derek and the Dominos
Delaney, Bonnie & Friends

Musician Carly Simon's father was **Richard Simon**, the co-founder of Simon & Schuster, Inc.

Bob Dylan was born Robert Zimmerman.

73 million viewers watched the debut appearance of the **Beatles on the Ed Sullivan Show** on February 9, 1964.

Muddy Waters's real name was McKinley Morganfield.

The famous opera house **La Scala** is in Milan, Italy.

Sting was born Gordon Matthew Sumner.

John Lennon was murdered by Mark David Chapman on December 8, 1980, in New York City.

A **soprano** is the highest female voice. An **alto** is the highest male voice. A **contralto** is the lowest female voice. A **bass** is the lowest male voice.

Duke Ellington's band was the house band at the **Cotton Club** in New York City from 1927 to 1931.

"Heartbreak Hotel" was Elvis Presley's first national number-one hit. The year was 1956.

Before they became the **"Fab Four,"** the Beatles were a quintet named the Silver Beatles. When guitarist Stu Sutcliffe left the band in 1961, the Beatles became a quartet.

Pete Best, who drummed for the Beatles starting in 1960, was replaced in April 1962 by Ringo Starr, the last member of the line-up.

The **Rock and Roll Hall of Fame and Museum** is in Cleveland, Ohio.

The first artists to be inducted into the **Rock and Roll Hall of Fame** in 1986 were:

Chuck Berry
James Brown
Ray Charles
Sam Cooke
Fats Domino
The Everly Brothers
Buddy Holly
Jerry Lee Lewis
Elvis Presley
Little Richard

Bobby Troup wrote the song "Route 66" in 1946 on a road trip going west to Los Angeles.

50 Cent's real name is Curtis Jackson.

Carnegie Hall in New York City opened on May 5, 1891.

Bands that played in the **1969 Woodstock Festival**:

Richie Havens
John B. Sebastian
Incredible String Band
Sweetwater
Bert Sommer
Tim Hardin
Ravi Shankar
Melanie
Arlo Guthrie
Joan Baez
Quill
Keef Hartley Band
Santana
Canned Heat
Mountain
Janis Joplin

Sly & The Family Stone
The Grateful Dead
Creedence Clearwater Revival
The Who
Jefferson Airplane
Joe Cocker
Country Joe & The Fish
Ten Years After
The Band
Blood Sweat and Tears
Johnny Winter
Crosby, Stills, Nash & Young
Paul Butterfield Blues Band
Sha-Na-Na
Jimi Hendrix

Iron Butterfly was scheduled to play **Woodstock** but got stuck at the airport.

Frank Sinatra always carried a roll of dimes with him after his son Frank Sinatra, Jr. was kidnapped (1963) and he used the dimes to call the kidnappers on the phone. His son was released unharmed.

The performer **Liberace** got his start playing the piano in bars in Milwaukee.

LANGUAGE

The most widely spoken language in the world is **Chinese** (Mandarin).

Annoying Clichés:

Words that have received the most nominations by the Plain English Campaign as the most irritating clichés in the language. The Campaign surveyed its 5,000 supporters in more than 70 countries as part of the build-up to its 25th anniversary in 2004.

Winner: "At the end of the day"
Second: "At this moment in time"
Third: "Like" used as punctuation
Fourth: "With all due respect"

The following terms also received **multiple nominations**:
24/7
absolutely
address the issue
around (in place of "about")
awesome
ballpark figure
basically
basis ("on a weekly basis" in place of "weekly" and so on)
bear with me
between a rock and a hard place
blue sky (thinking)
boggles the mind

bottom line
crack troops
diamond geezer
epicenter (used incorrectly)
glass half full (or half empty)
going forward
I hear what you're saying . . .
in terms of . . .
it's not rocket science
literally
move the goal-posts
ongoing
prioritize
pushing the envelope
singing from the same hymn sheet
the fact of the matter is
thinking outside the box
to be honest/to be honest with you/to be perfectly honest
touch base
up to (in place of "about")
value-added (in general use)

Bartholomew Gosnold gave **Cape Cod** its name because of the large amounts of cod caught there by his crew in 1602.

NASA stands for National Aeronautics and Space Administration.

DAYS OF THE WEEK IN SPANISH:

Monday	Lunes
Tuesday	Martes
Wednesday	Miércoles
Thursday	Jueves
Friday	Viernes
Saturday	Sábado
Sunday	Domingo

GROUPS OF ANIMALS ARE CALLED:

Alligators	Congregation
Bats	Colony
Cheetahs	Coalition
Crows	Murder
Doves	Dole
Gerbils	Horde
Gorillas	Band
Jellyfish	Smack
Owls	Parliament
Penguins	Rookery
Rhinos	Crash
Squirrels	Dray
Wombats	Warren

"Mile" comes from the Latin word *mille*, meaning one thousand.

The unabridged **Merriam-Webster Dictionary** has over 450,000 words.

The word **"posh"** originated from high-quality shipboard accommodations: portside out, starboard home.

The word **"blog"** is a shortened form of "web log."

B.C. (before Christ) stands for events before the birth of Jesus.

A.D. is short for the Latin phrase *Anno Domini*, translated as "in the year of our lord." It is used with dates to indicate the number of years passed since the birth of Jesus Christ.

a.k.a. stands for "also known as."

A, E, I, O, U are vowels in the alphabet. All remaining letters are consonants, although Y and W can sometimes double as vowels.

Hobson's choice refers to the idea of a choice that is offered when there is no real alternative; hence, there is no choice.

Free verse is verse without regular rhyme or meter.

Louis Braille, who was blind, developed the **Braille** alphabet that allows those without eyesight to read and write. It was first published in 1829 and refined in 1837.

A **limerick** has five lines.

The Latin term **mea culpa** means "my fault."

"e" is the most frequently used letter in the alphabet.

The letter **"o"** is said to be the oldest letter of the alphabet, originally used by the Egyptians.

Names that became words:

ALGORITHM: al-Khowarizmi (c. 800-c. 850), Arab mathematician

AUGUST: Augustus Caesar (63 B.C.-A.D. 14)

BAKELITE: Leo Hendrik Baekeland (1863-1944), Belgian-born American chemist

BIRO: József László Bíró (1899-1985), Hungarian inventor

BOYCOTT: Charles C. Boycott (1832-1897), English land agent

BUDDLEIA: Adam Buddle (c. 1660-1715), English rector and botanist

CAESAREAN SECTION: Gaius Julius Caesar, who according to legend was born in this manner

DERRICK: Goodman Derrick, a Tyburn hangman, circa 1600

DOBERMAN PINSCHER: Ludwig Dobermann, 19th century German dog breeder

DOILY: Mr. Doyley, a 17th century London draper

DRACONIAN: Draco, Athenian lawgiver, circa 650 B.C.

DUNCE: John Duns Scotus (c. 1265-1308), Scottish theologian

EPICURE: Epicurus (342-270 B.C.), Greek philosopher

FALLOPIAN TUBE: Gabriel Fallopius (1523-1562), Italian anatomist

FERRIS WHEEL: George Washington Gale Ferris (1859-1896), American engineer

FRISBEE: William Russell Frisbie, pie shop owner in Bridgeport CT

GALVANIZE: Luigi Galvani (1739-1798), Italian physiologist

HOBSON'S CHOICE: Thomas Hobson (1544-1631), English liveryman

JACUZZI: Roy Jacuzzi and Candido Jacuzzi (1903-1986), American inventors

LEOTARD: Jules Léotard (1839-1870), French acrobat

LUDDITE: Ned Ludd, 18th century Leicestershire, U.K. workman who destroyed machinery

MACKINTOSH: Charles Macintosh (1766-1843), inventor of the waterproofing process

MAGNOLIA: Pierre Magnol (1638-1715), French botanist

MASOCHISM: Leopold von Sacher-Masoch (1836-1895), Austrian novelist

MAUSOLEUM: Mausolus, 4th century B.C. King of Caria, Asia Minor

MAVERICK: Samuel Augustus Maverick (1803-1870), Texas cattle owner

MESMERIZE: Franz Anton Mesmer (1734-1815), Austrian physician

PASTEURIZE: Louis Pasteur (1822-1895), French chemist

POINSETTIA: Joel Roberts Poinsett (1779-1851), U.S. minister to Mexico

PYRRHIC: Pyrrhus (c. 318-272 B.C.), King of Epirus

SADISM: Count Donatien Alphonse François (Marquis) de Sade (1740-1814), French soldier and novelist

SAXOPHONE: Antoine-Joseph Sax, also known as Adolphe Sax (1814-1894), Belgian inventor

SHRAPNEL: Henry Shrapnel (1761-1842), British army officer

SILHOUETTE: Etienne de Silhouette (1709-1767), French minister of finance in 1759

TARMAC: John Loudon McAdam (1756-1836), Scottish engineer

TEDDY BEAR: Theodore Roosevelt (1858-1919), U.S. president

THESPIAN: Thespis, 6th century B.C. Greek playwright

ZEPPELIN: Count Ferdinand von Zeppelin (1838-1917), German general and aeronautical pioneer

A **Nobel laureate** is someone who has been awarded a Nobel Prize.

In a **court case**, the plaintiff brings the case to court. The defendant is the party against whom the case is brought.

The word **aphrodisiac** is named after the Greek goddess of love, Aphrodite.

The **"collective unconscious"** is used to explain ideas and memories shared by one culture.

A **tandem bicycle** is made for two. A so-called "tendem" bicycle has been made for ten.

The **Hebrew alphabet** has 22 letters.

The **$100 Hamburger** is aviation slang for a flight a pilot makes to dine at a non-local airport restaurant.

In ballet, a male dancer is called a **danseur**.

Proto-Indo-European (PIE) is considered the earliest source of several European languages. PIE is said to have been spoken about 5,000 years ago.

A **paralogical metaphor** has no resemblance between the idea and the image presented.

The term **"red herring"** (something meant to distract or mislead) comes from the old practice of using the scent from red (cured) herring fish to train hounds.

The term **beatnik** was coined by Herb Caen of the *San Francisco Chronicle* in 1958 as a derogatory term, derived from the Russian satellite Sputnik, to suggest that the beats were "way out there" and pro-Communist.

People who collect teddy bears are **archtophilists**.

In World War II, a **"Mae West"** was slang for a lifejacket.

A word or phrase that reads the same backwards and forwards is a **palindrome**.

HMO is an abbreviation for health maintenance organization.

The text of an opera is the **libretto**.

ZIP in **ZIP code** was named for Zoning Improvement Plan.

A monk or a priest in Tibetan Buddhism is known as a **lama**.

The symbol for **"and"** is an ampersand (&).

Attorney-client privilege refers to the understanding that what is said between an attorney and his/her client is confidential and cannot be used as evidence in a trial.

Onomatopoeia is the term we use for words that sound like what they are describing (e.g. "buzz," "meow").

The word **canine** (for a tooth) comes from the Latin *canis*, translated as "dog."

If you have **myopia**, you are nearsighted.

Montreal is the second-largest French-speaking city in the world. The first is Paris, France.

MISCELLANEOUS

The **Ceremony of the Keys** happens every night at the Tower of London at 10:00 p.m. The entrance gate and the Byward Tower are locked as part of a 30-minute ritual involving the famous question, "Halt, who goes there?" This tradition is said to be over 700 years old.

The **oldest tree on earth**, a bristlecone pine, was cut down by the United States Forest Service in Wheeler Peak, New Mexico, in 1964. The tree was 4,900 years old.

The **Boy Scouts of America** was founded on February 8, 1910.

The **Scripps National Spelling Bee** was started by the *Louisville Courier-Journal* in 1925. There were nine contestants.

WINNING WORDS FROM
THE SCRIPPS NATIONAL SPELLING BEE (1925-2005)

1925	gladiolus
1926	abrogate
1927	luxuriance
1928	albumen
1929	asceticism
1930	fracas
1931	foulard
1932	knack
1933	torsion
1934	deteriorating
1935	intelligible
1936	interning
1937	promiscuous
1938	sanitarium
1939	canonical
1940	therapy
1941	initials
1942	sacrilegious
1943-45	(No spelling bee due to WWII)
1946	semaphore
1947	chlorophyll
1948	psychiatry
1949	dulcimer
1950	meticulosity
1951	insouciant
1952	vignette
1953	soubrette
1954	transept
1955	crustaceology
1956	condominium
1957	schappe

1958	syllepsis
1959	catamaran
1960	eudaemonic
1961	smaragdine
1962	esquamulose
1963	equipage
1964	sycophant
1965	eczema
1966	ratoon
1967	chihuahua
1968	abalone
1969	interlocutory
1970	croissant
1971	shalloon
1972	macerate
1973	vouchsafe
1974	hydrophyte
1975	incisor
1976	narcolepsy
1977	cambist
1978	deification
1979	maculature
1980	elucubrate
1981	sarcophagus
1982	psoriasis
1983	purim
1984	luge
1985	milieu
1986	odontalgia
1987	staphylococci
1988	elegiacal
1989	spoliator
1990	fibranne
1991	antipyretic
1992	lyceum

1993	kamikaze
1994	antediluvian
1995	xanthosis
1996	vivisepulture
1997	euonym
1998	chiaroscurist
1999	logorrhea
2000	demarche
2001	succedaneum
2002	prospicience
2003	pococurante
2004	autochthonous
2005	appoggiatura

The **Barbie**® **doll** was based on a novelty doll named "Lilli" that was originally sold to gentlemen in Germany.

September 19th is **National Talk Like a Pirate Day**.

GENRE	AWARD
Television	Emmy
Film	Oscar
Broadway	Tony
Music	Grammy

American and **European children** watch an average of four hours of television per day.

The **Santa Cruz Beach Boardwalk** is the oldest running amusement park in California. It was founded in 1907.

Sir George Caley is credited with organizing the first-manned glider flight in Brompton, England in 1853. Orville and Wilbur Wright sent what is often deemed the first-manned flight up in 1903 near Kitty Hawk, North Carolina. Their flight is said to have lasted 59 seconds.

Sigmund Freud developed the idea of the Oedipus complex, in which the child feels attracted to the parent of the opposite sex and hostile toward the parent of the same sex. It was named after Oedipus, the Greek warrior who unknowingly slept with his mother in Sophocles's tragedy *Oedipus Rex*.

The cost of living in the United States is monitored in the **Consumer Price Index**, published each month by the federal government.

The **Leaning Tower of Pisa** in Italy is thought to have started leaning while it was being built.

Modern glass takes at least 4,000 years to decompose.

Mother Teresa, known for caring for the children of India, was born Agnes Gonxha Bojaxhiu in Albania. She lived from 1910-1997.

Russia was the first country to abolish capital punishment in 1826.

It is considered rude to talk with your hands on your hips in **Indonesia**.

The **Girl Scouts of America** was founded in 1912 in Savannah, Georgia.

Every **magnet** has two poles: north and south.

Ivory® soap floats.

The **first skyscraper** was built in 1885 in Chicago. The ten-story building was designed by William Le Baron Jenney.

The **United States Customs Service** was established on March 3, 1927.

There are over 9,000 miles of trails in the **United States National Trails System**.

Kwanza is celebrated from December 26 to January 1.

The **ancient Egyptians** were the first to use a solar calendar.

In Japan, only females present males with **Valentine's Day** gifts on February 14. On March 14, also known as "White Day," men give gifts.

Bonnie and Clyde's full names were Clyde Barrow and Bonnie Parker.

Famous advice columnists **Dear Abby** and **Ann Landers** were identical twins.

Christmas cards were first sent in London in 1843.

Sheets are marked by **thread count**, the number of threads in a square inch of fabric. The higher the count, the higher the quality (and price!) of the sheets.

A **"purl"** is a type of stitch in knitting.

Arthur Wynne is the father of the crossword puzzle.

Showers account for approximately 32% of home water use.

There are 120 different **Crayola® Crayon** colors. The 10 most popular colors are blue, cerulean, purple heart, midnight blue, aquamarine, Caribbean green, periwinkle, denim, cerise, and blizzard blue.

The eight **Crayola® Crayon** colors retired in 1990 were green blue, orange red, orange yellow, violet blue, maize, lemon yellow, blue gray, and raw umber.

Crayola® Crayons begin to soften at around 105° Fahrenheit, and they have a melting point between 128 and 147°.

The **world's longest kiss** took place on January 28, 2002. Louisa Almodovar and Rich Langly of New Jersey kissed for a record 30 hours, 59 minutes, and 27 seconds on a segment of *The Ricki Lake Show*.

The town of **Roswell**, New Mexico is said to have been the site of an alien spacecraft landing on July 4, 1947.

The **first kiss ever shown** in a movie was in 1896. The movie was called *The Kiss*.

In 1896 the **Farmer's Almanac** printed instructions for kissing, including "Take good aim."

Edward Brown, Jr. opened a drive/fly-in movie theater for cars and planes in 1948 in Asbury, New Jersey.

International Left-handers Day is August 13th.

The longest technical word in the English language, according to the *Oxford English Dictionary*, is **pneumonoultramicroscopicsilicovolcanoconiosis**. It is 45 letters long and refers to a type of lung disease.

The **Macy's Thanksgiving Day Parade**®, held annually in New York City, was started in 1924 by Macy's employees who were immigrants and wanted to celebrate American heritage.

The tallest species of tree in the United States is the **Coast Redwood,** found in Humboldt Redwoods State Park in California.

Yin and yang are the two forces in the universe in Chinese belief. Yin is the negative force; yang is the positive force.

Groundhog Day is February 2. It is said that if the groundhog sees its shadow on this day, there will be six more weeks of winter.

Russian cosmonaut **Valentina V. Tereshkova** was the first woman in space (1963).

It was French philosopher **René Descartes** who said, "I think, therefore I am."

Red, orange, yellow, green, blue, indigo, and violet are the colors of the **rainbow**.

BIRTHSTONES

January	Garnet
February	Amethyst
March	Aquamarine, Bloodstone
April	Diamond
May	Emerald
June	Pearl, Moonstone, Alexandrite
July	Ruby
August	Peridot, Sardonyx
September	Sapphire
October	Opal
November	Topaz
December	Turquoise

ASTROLOGICAL SIGNS

January 20 - February 18	Aquarius
February 19 - March 20	Pisces
March 21 - April 19	Aries
April 20 - May 20	Taurus
May 21- June 20	Gemini
June 21 - July 22	Cancer
July 23 - August 22	Leo
August 23 - September 22	Virgo
September 23 - October 22	Libra
October 23 - November 21	Scorpio
November 22 - December 21	Sagittarius
December 22 - January 19	Capricorn

STATE ABBREVIATIONS

Alabama	AL
Alaska	AK
Arizona	AZ
Arkansas	AR
California	CA
Colorado	CO
Connecticut	CT
Delaware	DE
Florida	FL
Georgia	GA
Hawaii	HI
Idaho	ID
Illinois	IL
Indiana	IN
Iowa	IA
Kansas	KS
Kentucky	KY
Louisiana	LA
Maine	ME
Maryland	MD
Massachusetts	MA
Michigan	MI
Minnesota	MN
Mississippi	MS
Missouri	MO
Montana	MT
Nebraska	NE
Nevada	NV
New Hampshire	NH
New Jersey	NJ
New Mexico	NM
New York	NY
North Carolina	NC
North Dakota	ND
Ohio	OH

Oklahoma	OK
Oregon	OR
Pennsylvania	PA
Rhode Island	RI
South Carolina	SC
South Dakota	SD
Tennessee	TN
Texas	TX
Utah	UT
Vermont	VT
Virginia	VA
Washington	WA
West Virginia	WV
Wisconsin	WI
Wyoming	WY

TRADITIONAL GIFTS FOR WEDDING ANNIVERSARIES:

YEAR	GIFT
First	Paper
Second	Cotton
Third	Leather
Fourth	Fruit, flowers
Fifth	Wood
Sixth	Sugar
Seventh	Copper, wool
Eighth	Bronze, pottery
Ninth	Pottery, willow
Tenth	Tin
Twentieth	China
Twenty-fifth	Silver
Thirtieth	Pearl
Fortieth	Ruby
Fiftieth	Gold
Sixtieth	Diamond
Seventieth	Platinum

The **first Thanksgiving** at Plymouth Rock lasted three days.

The **Winchester Mystery House**, a 160-room Victorian Mansion in San Jose, California, was the result of 38 years of continuous construction ordered by widow Sarah L. Winchester, an heiress to the Winchester Arms Company. Legend has it the widow was told by a medium that bad luck had plagued her and her family because of deaths from rifles made by the company and that she must move west. Winchester settled in San Jose and some say the continuous building of the house was suggested by the medium to confuse spirits. The house has 467 doorways, 1,257 windows, and 47 fireplaces.

Tuesday is considered an unlucky day in Greece.

It is unlucky to wear white at a **Chinese wedding**.

Filmmaker **Alfred Hitchcock** is said to have made cameo appearances in all of his films for good luck.

June is considered a good month to marry because the Roman goddess of marriage was **Juno**.

It is said that if you plant **lavender** around your house it will keep away bad luck and evil spirits.

If you see glass soda bottles on branches of a tree, it may be a **bottle tree**. The bottles are designed to capture evil spirits and keep them away from your house.

Admission to the **Smithsonian** museums and galleries in Washington D.C. is free.

In ancient Greece **parsley** was associated with death.

Places in England consider it a sign of war if **bees** have trouble producing honey.

It was once thought if shoes creaked, the **shoemaker** had not been paid.

A common belief is that if a **photo** falls from a wall (without reason), there will be a death of someone in the house.

In Britain a **black cat** is considered lucky. In the U.S. a black cat is considered unlucky.

The Pennsylvania Dutch believe that if a woman eats the last piece of bread, she will become an **"old maid."**

50% of the population of **Kenya** lives below the poverty line.

Mt. Saint Helen's in Washington State erupted on May 18, 1980.

In 1783, the **Pennsylvania Evening Post** became the first daily newspaper in America.

INDEX